JAVA

* * *

A Step-by-Step Guide for

Absolute Beginners

GUZZLER
MEDIA

Daniel Bell

Java: A Step-by-Step Guide For Absolute Beginners

Publisher: Amazon KDP & Guzzler Media LLC

GUZZLER
MEDIA

http://www.guzzlermedia.com
Contact: contact@guzzlermedia.com
Book and Cover design by Angela W.T.
ISBN: 9781699261699
Imprint: Independently published
First Edition: April 2019

CONTENTS

INTRODUCTION 1

1-GETTING STARTED WITH JAVA 3

What is Java?..3

Java Environment...4

First Java Program...5

2-JAVA CLASSES AND OBJECTS 9

Constructors...10

Creating Objects..11

Accessing Variables and Methods..12

3-VARIABLES IN JAVA 14

Variable Declaration..14

Variable Initialization..15

Variable Types...16

4-JAVA DATA TYPES..18

Primitive Data Types...18

Non-Primitive Data Types...20

Type Casting and Type Conversion.......................................21

5-ARRAYS IN JAVA..23

Single Dimensional Arrays...23

Multi-Dimensional Arrays...25

6-OPERATORS IN JAVA...27

Unary Operator..27

Arithmetic Operators...28

Logical Operators..29

Comparison Operators...30

7-DECISION MAKING STATEMENTS 33

if statement *33*

if...else statement *34*

if...else if...else Statement *36*

Nested if *38*

switch statement *39*

8-JAVA LOOPS..42

for Loop *42*

while Loop *44*

do...while Loop *45*

break Statement *47*

continue Statement *49*

9-JAVA METHODS 52

Creating Methods *52*

Calling Methods *54*

The void Keyword *56*

Call by Value *56*

Abstract Methods *58*

Method Overloading *59*

Command-Line Arguments *61*

The this Keyword *62*

Variable Arguments *64*

Method Overriding *66*

Recursive Functions in Java *69*

10-INHERITANCE IN JAVA 73

Single Inheritance *75*

Multilevel Inheritance *76*

Hierarchical Inheritance *77*

Invoking Superclass Constructor *79*

The instance of Keyword *80*

11-ABSTRACTION IN JAVA **82**

12-ENCAPSULATION **88**

13-INTERFACES **92**

14-PACKAGES **97**

Import Keyword *100*

15-JAVA APPLETS **104**

Applets' Lifecycle *104*

Displaying Images *110*

Applet Animations *112*

Events on Applets *113*

Applet Parameters *115*

16-JAVA INPUT/ OUTPUT **118**

Byte Streams *118*

Character Streams *119*

Standard Streams *121*

Reading and Writing Files *123*

File Navigation *125*

Listing Directories *130*

17-EXCEPTION HANDLING **131**

Catching Exceptions *133*

Multiple Catch Blocks *134*

Throw/Throws Keywords *135*

Finally Statement *137*

Try-with-resources *138*

User-defined Exceptions *140*

18-JAVA AWT **144**

Handling Events *147*

AWT Button *151*

AWT Label *153*

AWT TextField *156*

AWT TextArea *160*

AWT Checkbox *162*

AWT CheckboxGroup *165*

AWT Menu and MenuItem *168*

KeyListener Interface *169*

CONCLUSION **172**

ABOUT THE AUTHOR **174**

ACKNOWLEDGMENTS **175**

Introduction

Java is a great programming language that can be used for the development of both standalone and distributed applications. These types of applications are on high demand today for both small and large enterprises. Java comes with a feature known as apples which are web pages that can be embedded on web browsers. This means that Java can help you add some functionality to your web applications. You can now tell why Java is a popular programming language with a high demand worldwide. It also has many other features which you can take advantage of when developing your application. For instance, Java is an object-oriented programming language. If you are familiar with any other object-oriented programming language, it will be easy for you to learn Java. Java has a simple syntax easy to grasp, even by beginners.

It is easy to get started with writing and running Java programs. You only need to have the Java compiler installed on your computer and a text editor where you will write your code. With these, you can write your Java programs and get instant results. For the case of the text editor, a basic text editor like Notepad is okay although there are more advanced text editors for Java-like NetBeans and Eclipse. Once you compile your Java code, you get the Java byte-code which is platform independent, meaning you can execute it on a machine running any type of operating system. This book is an excellent guide for you to learn everything about Java. The author takes you from the initial steps of getting started with Java to develop your own Java application. Enjoy reading!

1-Getting Started with Java

What is Java?

Java is both a platform and a programming language. As a platform, we have the Java runtime environment (JRE) which is a software environment on which programs can run. As a language, Java is a high-level, robust and object-oriented programming language. The language was developed by Suns Microsystems in 1995.

Since Java is an object-oriented programming language, it treats everything as an object. The object model nature of the language also makes it easy for us to extend it. Java programs go through two steps to generate results. The first step is compilation after which the Java bytecode is generated. The Java bytecode is platform independent, meaning that it can be run on any machine. After the compilation, the bytecode is passed through the execution step to generate the results.

Java is known to be an easy language. If you are familiar with the concepts of object-oriented programming, then it will be easy for you to understand Java. Java comes with a secure feature that allows developers to create temper-free and virus-free systems. The public-key encryption is used as a technique for securing the systems.

Java Environment

To write and running your Java programs, you must have the Java compiler and a text editor such as Notepad in Windows. To get the Java compiler, you must install the Java Development (JDK) on your computer. Once this is installed, your computer will have the Java compiler.

Now you have the Java compiler, you must have a text editor in which you will write your programs. You can use either a basic text editor or an advanced text editor. Examples of advanced text editors you can use for Java programming include NetBeans and Eclipse. You can download the JDK from the following

URL:**http://www.oracle.com/technetwork/java/javase/downloa ds/jdk8-downloads-2133151.html**

Once the download is complete, just double click the setup file and the installation process will begin. You will be taken through a sequence of simple on-screen instructions for the installation to be done. Installation alone is not enough as you have to do something for the Java installation directories to be known. You have to set the path environment variable. This way, you will be able to invoke the Java compiler from the terminal of your operating system. In most cases, the installation of JDK is done in the c:\Program Files\java\jdk directory. On windows, you can set the path environment variable by right clicking **"My Computer"** then choosing **"Properties"**. Next, open the **"Advanced"** tab then choose **"Environment variables"**. Add the **"c:\Program Files\java\jdk\bin"** path. Linux users are advised to read the documentation of their shells.

First Java Program

We need to create the Hello World Java example. To do this, open your text editor such as Notepad and create a new file. Give this file the name Hello.java. Mark the directory where you save this file. Add the following java code to the file and save it:

```java
public class Hello {

    /* my first java program
     * the code will print 'Hello World'
     */

    public static void main(String []args) {
        System.out.println("Hello World"); // to print
Hello World
    }
}
```

Once you have saved the above code, open the terminal of your operating system and navigate to the directory where you have saved the file.

Run the following command on the terminal:

```
javac Hello.java
```

The above command should generate the *Hello.class* file. This is the file with the Java byte code, which is platform-independent. You can confirm this by checking the same directory for this file. What we have done is that we have invoked the Java compiler (Jayac) on the file to compile the Java code contained in the file.

Now that the code has compiled with no error, we can execute it. Just run the following command on the same terminal:

```
java Hello
```

The above command should return results on the terminal as shown below:

```
C:\Windows\system32>cd C:\Users\admin

C:\Users\admin>javac Hello.java

C:\Users\admin>java Hello
Hello World

C:\Users\admin>
```

The above output shows that the code returned *Hello World* as the output.

Consider the following line which I have extracted from the code:

```
public class Hello {
```

6

What we are doing in the above line is that we are creating a class named *Hello*. The *H* in the class name has been written in uppercase; hence we must write the class that way anytime we are referring to it. Java is a case sensitive language. The public is an access modifier, declaring the class as public, meaning it can be accessed from the rest of the classes contained within the same package. The opening curly brace { marks the beginning of the body of the class and to close it, we must use the closing curly brace }.

Consider the following section extracted from the code:

```
/* my first java program
   * the code will print 'Hello World'
   */
```

The above is a comment. Note that we have enclosed them within /* and */. This is the way we denote block comments in Java. Comments can also be a single line, and such are denoted using two forward slashes //. Here is an example:

```
// my first java program
```

The Java compiler does nothing to comment, but it skips them. Comments improve the readability of the code. They are used to give explanations on what the various lines of code should do.

Note that the file was given the name *Hello.java*, and the class was given the name *Hello*. If these two don't match this way, an error will be generated. This should always be the case when you want to run your Java code from the terminal of your operating system.

Here is another line extracted from the code:

```
public static void main(String args[]){
```

The above is referred to as the main method. No Java program can run or execute without the main method. Here is another line extracted from the code:

```
System.out.println("Hello World");
```

We have called a method named **println** to help us print the text we pass to it on the display. You have also noticed that we have used two closing curly braces }}. The first one closes the main method while the second one closes the class.

2-Java Classes and Objects

As we had stated, Java is an object-oriented programming language. This means it can support the various concepts of the object-oriented programming paradigm.

In Java, objects are characterized by states and behaviors. An example of an object is a dog. Some of its states that characterize it include name, color, and breed. Some behaviors that characterize it include eating, barking and wagging of the tail. An object is an instance of a class.

A class is a template or blueprint that describes the state and behavior that any object of its type should support. Here is an example of a class:

```
public class Dog {
```

```
String name;
int breed;
String color;

void eating() {
}

void barking() {
}

void sleeping() {
}
}
```

In the above example, we have defined a class named **Dog**. Three variables have been defined inside this class, which are the **name**, **breed**, and **color**. These are the properties of the **Dog class**. We have also defined **3** methods for the class. These are **eating()**, **barking()** and **sleeping()**. We can define many methods inside a class.

Constructors

Constructors are important parts of classes. Each class has a constructor. If you don't create a class constructor explicitly, the Java compiler will automatically initialize a default constructor for the class.

Every time you create a new object, at least a single constructor will be invoked. Note that there is a rule that governs the definition and use of constructors in Java. A constructor must have the same name as a class. A class may have over one constructor.

Here is an example:

```
public class Dog {
    public Dog() {
    }

    public Dog(String breed) {
        // A constructor with one parameter, breed.
    }
}
```

In the above class, we have created two constructors, one without arguments and another one with one argument. You should note that the two constructors share the same name with the class.

Creating Objects

The purpose of a class is to provide a template or a blueprint from which we will create objects. This means that objects are created from classes. In Java, objects are created using the new keyword. The following sequence of steps should be followed when creating Java objects:

1. Declaration- this should involve declaring a variable with an object type.

2. Instantiation- this is the creation of an object using the new keyword.

3. Initialization- the new keyword is normally followed by calling the constructor. This will initialize the new object.

The following example shows how an object can be created:

```
public class Dog {
```

```
    public Dog(String breed) {
        // A constructor with one parameter, breed
        System.out.println("You passed the breed :" +
breed );
    }

    public static void main(String []args) {
        // Creating an object puppy
        Dog puppy = new Dog( "Poodle" );
    }
}
```

Upon execution, the code will return:

```
You passed the breed :Poodle
```

From the *class Dog*, we could create an object named *puppy*.

Accessing Variables and Methods

In classes, one of the best ways for us to access instance variables and methods is by creating objects. An instance variable can be accessed by following the sequence of steps given below:

```
/* Begin by creating an object */
ObjectReference = new Constructor();

/* Next, call the variable */
ObjectReference.variableName;

/* Call a class method */
ObjectReference.MethodName();
```

Here is an example showing this:

```java
public class Dog {
    String name;

    public Dog(String breed) {
        // A constructor with one parameter, breed.
        System.out.println("You passed the breed :" +
breed );
    }

    public void setName( String puppyName ) {
        name = puppyName;
    }

    public String getName( ) {
        System.out.println("Puppy's name is :" + name
);

        return name;
    }

    public static void main(String []args) {
        /* Object creation */
        Dog puppy = new Dog( "poodle" );

        /* Call class method and set puppy's name */
        puppy.setName( "Tommy" );

        /* Call another class method and get puppy's
name */
        puppy.getName( );

        /* Instance variables can also be accessed as
follows */
        System.out.println("Variable Value :" +
puppy.name );
    }
}
```

The code will return the following output upon execution:

```
You passed the breed :poodle
Puppy's name is :Tommy
Variable Value :Tommy
```

3-Variables in Java

A *variable* can be seen as a container responsible for holding value during the life of a program. Each variable is of a certain data type, designative the value it can hold. There are two steps in using Java variables: **variable declaration**, and **variable initialization**.

Variable Declaration

The declaration of a variable involves giving it a name and specifying its data type. Below are examples of valid variable declaration:

```
int a, x, p;

float pi;

double p;

char c;
```

The ***int***, ***float***, ***double*** and ***char*** are the data types, specifying the value each variable can or should hold. To declare several variables in one line, separate them using a comma (,) as in the first example. A variable declaration should end with a semicolon (;).

Variable Initialization

Variable initializing involves assigning it a valid value. The value to be assigned to the variable is determined by the data type the variable is **of**. Below are examples of valid variable initializations.

```
pi =3.14f;

a =10.12768781;

c= 's';
```

Both declaration and initialization of a variable can be done at once as shown below:

```
int a=1, x=4, p=5;
float pi=3.14f;
```

```
double p=15.23d;

char c= 's';
```

Variable Types

Java supports three variable types:

1. **Local Variables**

2. **Static Variables**

3. **Instance Variables**

Local Variables

These are variables declared within a method body. They can only be accessed from within that method.

Instance Variables

These are the variables that have been defined without the use of a STATIC keyword. These variables are specific to an object.

Static Variables

These are variables initialized once and at the beginning of program execution. You should initialize them before instance variables.

The following example shows the different *Java variables*:

```
class VariablesExample {
    int p = 1; //an instance variable
    static int q = 5; //a static variable
    void methodExample() {
        int r = 10; //a local variable
    }
}
```

The variable *integer q* is a static variable since it has been defined with the *static keyword*. The variable *int r* has been declared within the *methodExample* method, making it a local variable. It can only be accessed from within that method.

4-Java Data Types

In Java, a data type can be primitive or non-primitive.

Primitive Data Types

These are the pre-defined data types that are already provided by Java. They are **8** in number including *byte*, *short*, *long*, *char*, *int*, *float*, *Boolean* and *double* data types.

Let us now discuss the various primitive data types in Java:

Boolean

This data type stores only two values, which are *true* and *false*. It is used in simple statements that track only **true/false conditions**.

It specifies only one bit of information, but we cannot define its size precisely.

Byte

This has a default value of **0**, and its minimum value is **-128 (-2^7)**. It helps in saving space in large arrays as it is 4 times smaller than integers.

Short

It has a default value of **0** and values lying with the range of -**32,768** to **32,767**. It can also be used for saving on space just like the byte data type.

Int

This also has a default value of **0** and values ranging between -**2,147,483,648** and **2,147,483,647**. It has a minimum value of -**2,147,483,648** and a maximum value of **2,147,483,647**.

Long

This data type also has a default value of **0** with its values ranging between **-9,223,372,036,854,775,808** and **9,223,372,036,854,775,807**. Its minimum value is -**9,223,372,036,854,775,808** while its maximum value is **9,223,372,036,854,775,807**. It is the best data type to use when you want to have a long range of values than the o0nes provided by the *int* data type.

Float

This data type has an unlimited range of values. It can help you save on space compared to the use of a double. Avoid using this data type for precise values like currency. Its default value is **0.0F**.

Double

This data type has a default value of **0.0d** and it comes with an unlimited range of values. It used to represent values with the decimal part just like the float data type. Avoid using it for precision values like currency.

Char

This data type is used for storing characters.

Non-Primitive Data Types

These are defined by the use of the defined class constructors. They help programmers' access objects. They include Strings and arrays.

The example given below shows the use of variables:

```java
public class AddVarriables{
    public static void main(String[] args){
    int p=10;
    int q=22;
    int r=p+q;
    System.out.println(r);
    }
}
```

We have defined three integer variables *p,q,* and *r*. The values for *p* and *q* have been initialized, while the value for *r* is the addition of the previous two variables. We have then invoked the println function to print the value of *r*. It should print **32**, the result of the addition of **10** and **22**. This is shown below:

32

Type Casting and Type Conversion

It is possible for a variable of a particular type to get a value of some other type. Type conversion is when a variable of a smaller capacity is assigned a variable of a bigger capacity.

Example:

```
double p;
int q=6;
p-q;
```

Typecasting is when a variable of larger capacity is assigned some other variable of a smaller capacity.

Example:

```
p =6;
int q;
q= (int) p;
```

The *(int)* is known as the *type cast operator*. If it is not specified you get an error. Typecasting example:

```
public class TypecastingExample{
public static void main(String[] args){
float p=19.7f;
//int q=p;//a compile time error
int q=(int)p;
System.out.println(p);
System.out.println(q);
}
}
```

The code returns the following upon execution:

```
19.7
19
```

5-Arrays in Java

Arrays are storage structures used for storing same-type elements. An array has a fixed size, which cannot be increased after definition. The first element in an array is at index **0**.

Single Dimensional Arrays

These are arrays in which the elements are stored linearly. The declaration of an array takes the syntax given below:

```
<elementDataType>[] <arrayName>;
```

Another syntax:

```
<elementDataType> <arrayName>[];
```

Example:

```
int arrayExample[];
int []arrayExample;
```

An array can be initialized as follows

```
arrayExample[0]=20;
```

The line states that the element **1** should be stored at index **0** of the array. An array can also be declared and initialized simultaneously:

```
int arrayExample[] = {19, 21, 34, 87};
```

The value 10 will be stored at index 0 of the array, 21 at index 1 and so on.

Example:

```
public class JavaArrayExample{
    public static void main(String args[]){
        int myarr[] = new int[15];
        for (int p=0;p<15;p++){
            myarr[p]=p+1;
        }
        for (int p=0;p<15;p++){
            System.out.println("myarr"+p+"] =
"+myarr[p]);
        }
    System.out.println("The Array Length  =
"+myarr.length);

    }
}
```

The array will print the elements contained at different indices as shown below:

```
myarr0]  = 1
myarr1]  = 2
myarr2]  = 3
myarr3]  = 4
myarr4]  = 5
myarr5]  = 6
myarr6]  = 7
myarr7]  = 8
myarr8]  = 9
myarr9]  = 10
myarr10] = 11
myarr11] = 12
myarr12] = 13
myarr13] = 14
myarr14] = 15
The Array Length  =  15
```

We also got the length of the array, which is **15**.

Multi-Dimensional Arrays

These can be seen as arrays of other arrays. In a multi-dimensional array declaration, you only add another set of square brackets to define the other index. Example:

```
int arr2[ ][ ] = new int[12][45] ;
```

You have the authority to control the length of your multi-dimensional array.

Example:

```
public class JavaArrayExample2 {
public static void main(String[] args) {

// Creating a 2-dimensional array.
   int arr2[ ][ ] = new int[12][45] ;
   // Assign only three elements
   arr2[0][0] = 0;
   arr2 [1][1] = 12;
   arr2 [3][2] = 23;
```

25

```
    System.out.println(arr2[0][0] + " ");
    System.out.println(arr2[1][1] + " ");
  }
}
```

The program will return the value stored at index **[0][0]** and index

[1][1] as shown below:

```
          0
          12
```

6-Operators in Java

Operators are symbols used to perform operations. For example, the + symbol is used for arithmetic operations. Java supports different operators:

Unary Operator

This is an operator that takes one operand. They increment/decrement a value. They include ++ **(increment)** and - - **(decrement).**

Example:

```
public class JavaUnaryOperator{
public static void main(String args[]){
```

```
int p=0;
System.out.println(p++);//from 0 to 1
System.out.println(++p);//2
System.out.println(p--);//1
System.out.println(--p);//0
}
}
```

The program prints the following after execution:

```
0
2
2
0
```

The **p++** means that the value of **p** is read first before the increment is done; hence we got the value of **p** as **0**. If it was **++p**, then we would get a 1 as the first value of p. You can try it.

Arithmetic Operators

These operators are used for performing mathematical operations like multiplication, addition, division, subtraction, etc. They are used as mathematical operators.

Example:

```
public class ArithmeticOperators{
public static void main(String args[]){
int p=13;
int q=4;
System.out.println(p+q); //17
System.out.println(p-q); //9
System.out.println(p*q); //52
System.out.println(p/q); //3
System.out.println(p%7); //6
}
```

}

The code returns the following result upon execution:

```
17
9
52
3
6
```

We have two integer variables p and q with their respective values initialized. We have got the *addition, subtraction, multiplication, and division* of these variables. The division ignores the decimal part as the variables have been declared as integers rather than floats or doubles. The only operator that may look unfamiliar is the % (**modulus operator**), which returns the rest after division.

Logical Operators

These operators are used together with binary values. They help in the evaluation of conditions in loops and conditional statements. They include ||, **&&**, !. Suppose we have two Boolean variable **a1** and **a2,** the following conditions apply:

• **a1&&a2** will return true if both **a1** and **a2** are true, otherwise, false.

• **a1||a2** will return false if both **a1** and **a2** are false, otherwise true.

• **!a1** will return the opposite of **a1**.

Example:

```
public class JavaLogicalOperator {
```

```
public static void main(String args[]) {
    boolean p = true;
    boolean q = false;

    System.out.println("p && q: " + (p&&q));
    System.out.println("p || q: " + (p||q));
    System.out.println("!(p && q): " + !(p&&q));
}
}
```

The program will return the following upon execution:

```
p && q: false
p || q: true
!(p && q): true
```

The value of variable *p* has been set to *true* while that of variable *q* has been set to a *false*. In the first case, we are using *&& operator*, hence *true* and *false* return a *false*. In the second case, we are using the || **operator**, hence *true* or *false* give a *true*. In the last case, we are negating the result of the *&& operation*.

Comparison Operators

Java supports 6 types of comparison operators, ==, !=, <, >, >=, <=:

- == will return true if both left and right sides are equal.

- != will return true if the left and right sides of the operator are not equal.

- \> returns true if the left side is greater than the right side.

- \< returns true if the left side is less than the right side.

- \>= returns true if the left side is greater than/equal to the right.

- <= returns true if the left side is less than the right side.

Example:

```
public class RelationalOperator {
    public static void main(String args[]) {
        int p = 10;
        int q = 15;
        if (p==q) {
        System.out.println("p and q are equal");
        }
        else{
        System.out.println("p and q aren't equal");
        }

        if( p != q ){
        System.out.println("p and q aren't equal");
        }
        else{
        System.out.println("p and q are equal");
        }

        if( p > q ){
        System.out.println("p is greater than q");
        }
        else{
        System.out.println("p isn't greater than q");
        }

        if( p >= q ){
        System.out.println("p is equal to or greater
than q");
        }
        else{
        System.out.println("p is less than q");
        }

        if( p < q ){
```

```
       System.out.println("p is less than q");
         }
       else{
       System.out.println("p isn't less than q");
         }

         if( p <= q){
       System.out.println("p is equal to or less than
q");
         }
       else{
       System.out.println("p is greater than q");
         }
      }
}
```

The code should return the following result after execution:

```
p and q aren't equal
p and q aren't equal
p isn't greater than q
p is less than q
p is less than q
p is equal to or less than q
```

We have used various comparison operators to compare the values of variables *p* and *q*.

7-Decision Making Statements

In Java, decision making helps us to test conditions and run statements based on the outcome of the condition. Let us discuss the statements for decision making:

if statement

This statement has a ***Boolean expression*** and ***statement(s)***. Its syntax is given below:

```
if(A_boolean_expression) {
    // Statement(s) to be run if true
```

}

The statements within the body of the expression will run if the condition is true, otherwise, no result from the program.

Example:

```java
public class JavaIfStatement {

    public static void main(String args[]) {
        int x = 5;

        if( x < 10 ) {
            System.out.print("The value of x is below
10");
        }
    }
}
```

The code will return the following result upon execution:

```
The value of x is below 10
```

We have declared a variable named **x** and initialized its value to **5**. In the *if* condition; we are checking whether the value of this variable is below **10**. Since this is *true*, the statement below this condition has been executed.

if...else statement

This statement combines an *"if"* with *"else"*, with the latter specifying the statement(s) to run if the expression is false. Syntax:

```
if(A_boolean_expression) {
    // Statement(S) to run if expression is true
}else {
    // Statement(s) to run if expression is false
}
Example:
public class JavaIfElseStatement {

    public static void main(String args[]) {
        int marks = 30;

        if( marks < 50 ) {
            System.out.print("The marks is below 50");
        }else {
            System.out.print("The marks is above 50");
        }
    }
}
```

The first statement will be printed, **the marks are below 50**. This is because the Boolean expression will be *true*. If it is *false*, the other statement will be printed.

Example:

```
public class JavaIfElseStatement {

    public static void main(String args[]) {
        int x = 10;

        if( x < 5 ) {
            System.out.print("The value of x is below
5");
        }else {
            System.out.print("The value of x is above
5");
        }
    }
}
```

The code returns the following execution:

```
The value of x is above 5
```

The value of variable, **x** has been set to **10**. In the **if condition**, we are checking whether this value is below **5**. This will test to a *false*, hence the *else* part will be executed.

if...else if...else Statement

If you have several conditions to test, use this statement. Syntax

```
if(A_boolean_expression a) {
    // Statement(s)
}else if(A_boolean_expression b) {
    // Statement(s)
}else if(A_boolean_expression c) {
    // Statement(s)
}else {
    // Statement(s)
}
```

Example:

```
public class JavaIfElseIfStatement {

    public static void main(String args[]) {
        int x = 15;
```

```
    if( x == 10 ) {
        System.out.print("value of x is 10");
    }else if( x == 15 ) {
        System.out.print("value of x is 15");
    }else if( x == 20 ) {
        System.out.print("value of x is 20");
    }else {
        System.out.print("None of the above");
    }
}
}
```

The code gives the following result after execution:

```
value of x is 15
```

The value of variable **x** was initialized to **15**, hence the test condition for **15** tested to a *true*. The statement below was executed to give us the above result.

Here is another example:

```
public class JavaIfElseIfStatement {
public static void main(String[] args) {
    int marks=64;

    if(marks<40){
        System.out.println("You fail");
    }
    else if(marks>=40 && marks<50){
        System.out.println("You scored D grade");
    }
    else if(marks>=50 && marks<60){
        System.out.println("You scored C grade");
    }
    else if(marks>=60 && marks<70){
```

37

```
            System.out.println("You scored B grade");
    }
    else if(marks>=70){
            System.out.println("You scored A grade");
}
}
}
```

The code returns the following upon execution:

```
You scored B grade
```

The value of variable **marks** is **64,** hence it lies between **60** and **70.** The **else if** the condition for that will test to a **true** hence the statement within its body will be executed.

N e s t e d   i f

The **if...else** statements can be nested, meaning that one may use an if inside another **if** or an **if...else** inside another **if...else**.

The nesting the syntax is shown below:

```
if(A_boolean_expression a) {
    // Statament(s)
    if(A_boolean_expression b) {
        // Statament(s)
    }
}
```

Example:

```
public class NestingExample {
```

```
public static void main(String args[]) {
    int age=32;
    int weight=77;

    if(age>=18){
        if(weight>55){
            System.out.println("You can donate
blood.");
        }
    }
}
}
```

The code prints the following result upon execution:

```
You can donate blood.
```

If the first condition becomes *true*, the second condition will test. This is true in our case; hence the *println* statement was executed. If any of the conditions is *false*, then the *println* statement will not be executed. This means that for the *println* statement to be executed, all the conditions must test to a *true*.

switch statement

This statement allows us to test a certain variable for equality against some values list. Every value is referred to as a *case*.

The following syntax is used:

```
switch(an_expression) {
    case value:
        // Statement(s)
```

```
        break; //optional

    case value:
        // Statement(s)
        break; //optional

    default : //Optional
        // Statement(s)
}
```

The switch will end once it has reached the **break** statement. The flow will then jump to the next line. However, note that there is not an obligation to add a **break** to every *case*. A ***default case*** may add to the end of the *switch*, and this will run ***if none of the cases is true***.

Example:

```java
public class JavaSwitchExample {

    public static void main(String args[]) {
        char your_grade = 'A';

        switch(your_grade) {
            case 'A':
                System.out.println("That is Excellent!");
                break;
            case 'B':
                System.out.println("That is Good!");
                break;
            case 'C':
                System.out.println("That is Fair!");
                break;
            case 'D':
                System.out.println("That is Poor!");
            case 'F':
                System.out.println("You Failed!");
                break;
            default:
                System.out.println("Unknown grade");
        }
```

```
    System.out.println("You scored " + your_grade);
  }
}
```

The code returns the result given below:

```
That is Excellent!
You scored A
```

The *case* for grade **A** tested to a *true*, hence the source of the above output.

The last *println* statement will execute in all cases regardless of the value of the grade.

8-Java Loops

Java loops help us do some tasks repeatedly. Loops execute the statements in a sequential manner. The first one is run first, followed by second, etc. Let us discuss the various types of loops supported in Java:

for Loop

The loop is run provided condition tests to true. The execution will stop immediately the condition becomes false. Syntax:

```
for(initialization; loop_condition ;
Increment/decrement_part)
{
    the_statement(s);
}
```

The *initialization* defines the initial value of the loop condition. The *loop_condition* specifies the condition that must always be true for loop to run. The *loop_increment/decrement* defines the amount by which the initialization value will be incremented or decremented after any iteration. Example:

```
public class ForLoopExample {
    public static void main(String args[]){
        for(int p=0; p<10; p++){
            System.out.println("The value of p now
is: "+p);
        }
    }
}
```

The program returns the following as the output:

```
The value of p now is: 0
The value of p now is: 1
The value of p now is: 2
The value of p now is: 3
The value of p now is: 4
The value of p now is: 5
The value of p now is: 6
The value of p now is: 7
The value of p now is: 8
The value of p now is: 9
```

The output shows that the loop returns the values of variable *p* from **0** to **9**. When the *loop* increments the **9** to get **10**, it will find that it is violating the *loop* condition, **p<10**, hence the execution will stop immediately.

while Loop

This loop executes the statement(s) as long as the specified condition is *true*. The condition is first tested and if true, the *loop statement(s)* are executed. If the condition becomes *false*, control will jump to execute statements that come after the loop. It is recommended you add an increment/decrement to the loop and a *test* condition so that the loop stops execution when the condition becomes **false**. Otherwise, the loop may run indefinitely.

Syntax:

```
while(A_boolean_expression) {
    // Statement(s)
}
Example:
public class JavaWhileLoopExample {

    public static void main(String args[]) {
        int p = 5;

        while( p < 12 ) {
            System.out.print("The value of p is: " + p
);
            p++;
            System.out.print("\n");
        }
    }
}
```

The code prints the following result:

```
The value of p is: 5
The value of p is: 6
The value of p is: 7
The value of p is: 8
The value of p is: 9
The value of p is: 10
The value of p is: 11
```

The program prints **p**'s value from **5** to **11**. The variable's initial value is **5**. The **test** condition checks whether this value is **less** than **12**, which is **true**. This means the loop will run. When it reached **11**, it will check and find the value of **p** is **12**. The execution of the loop then stops immediately since continuing to execute it will violate the **loop** condition.

d o ... w h i l e L o o p

This is closely related to the while loop. In the *while loop* condition, execution is done before loop body execution. This is the opposite in *do...while loop* as the body is executed first *before* the condition. In *while loop*, the loop body may *never* be executed, but in *do...while loop*, the loop body *must be executed for at least once*.

Syntax:

```
do
{
    Statement or statements;
} while(loop_condition);
Example:
public class JavaDoWhileLoop {

    public static void main(String args[]) {
        int p = 5;
```

```
        do {
            System.out.print("The value of p is: " + p
);
            p++;
            System.out.print("\n");
        }while( p < 12 );
    }
}
```

The code will print the value of **p** from **5** to **11** just as in the previous loop. This is because the *condition is true*, **5** is less than **12**. Suppose we set loop condition as *false*, for example, initialize the value of **p** to **20** as shown below:

```
public class JavaDoWhileLoop {

    public static void main(String args[]) {
        int p = 20;

        do {
            System.out.print("The value of p is: " + p
);
            p++;
            System.out.print("\n");
        }while( p < 12 );
    }
}
```

After running the above program, you will get the following output:

```
The value of p is: 20
```

This means that the while condition is *false*. This is because the

Java compiler first runs through the program for the initial value of *p* which is **20**. That value is printed. Once it moves to loop condition, it violates the condition, *p<20*, hence **loop execution** stops immediately.

There are two statements that are used for controlling how Java loops are executed. They are called *continue* and *break* statements. They work by changing the normal way of executing a loop.

Let us discuss them.

break Statement

This statement causes the execution of a loop to a halt, and control jumps to the statement that comes next after the loop. It also stops a case in a *switch* statement.

Syntax:

```
your-jump-statement;
break;
Example:
public class BreakStatementExample {
public static void main(String[] args) {
    for(int p=0;p<=10;p++){
        if(p==0){
            break;
        }
        System.out.println("The value of p is:" +p);
    }
}
}
```

The program will print the following after execution:

```
The value of p is:0
The value of p is:1
The value of p is:2
The value of p is:3
The value of p is:4
The value of p is:5
```

This is because of the following section of our program:

```
if(p==6){
        break;
```

The increment is done from **0** to **5**, and once it notices that the value of p is **6**, it will halt immediately as it will violate the above condition. For the case of *nested* loops, the *break* can be added to the inner loop and it *will* break it. This *will* cause the inner loop to break once the specified condition is met.

Example:

```
public class BreakStatementExample2 {
    public static void main(String[] args) {
            for(int p=1;p<=5;p++){
                    for(int q=1;q<=5;q++){
                        if(p==3&&q==3){
                            break;
                        }
                        System.out.println(p+"
"+q);
                    }
            }
        }
    }
```

The code will print the following as the result:

```
1 1
1 2
1 3
1 4
1 5
2 1
2 2
2 3
2 4
2 5
3 1
3 2
4 1
4 2
4 3
4 4
4 5
5 1
5 2
5 3
5 4
5 5
```

When the Java compiler finds that both the values of **p** and **q** are **3**, it will skip and move to the next values.

continue Statement

This statement makes the loop jump to next iteration immediately. It helps the loop to continue after a jump. Note that in the previous case, the loop halted immediately. This statement can help it resume execution in the next iteration after the jump.

Example:

```
your_jump-statement;
continue;
```

Example:

```
public class JavaContinueStatamentExample {
public static void main(String[] args) {
    for(int p=10;p<=20;p++){
        if(p==15){
            continue;
        }
        System.out.println("The value of p is:" +p);
    }
  }
}
```

The code gives the following result:

```
The value of p is:10
The value of p is:11
The value of p is:12
The value of p is:13
The value of p is:14
The value of p is:16
The value of p is:17
The value of p is:18
The value of p is:19
The value of p is:20
```

All values between **10** and **20** have been printed except **15**. The *continue* statement may also be used with an **inner** loop. In such a case, it will only continue your *inner* loop.

Example:

```
public class JavaContinueStatament2 {
 public static void main(String[] args) {
            for(int p=1;p<=3;p++){
                    for(int q=1;q<=3;q++){
                        if(p==2&&q==2){
                            continue;
                        }
                        System.out.println(p+"
"+q);
                    }
            }
    }
}
```

The code returns the following result:

```
1 1
1 2
1 3
2 1
2 3
3 1
3 2
3 3
```

9-Java Methods

In Java, **methods** are used for grouping a set of statements for the purpose of performing the same function. A good example of a function is the **System.out.println**. This method is in built in Java. When you call the above method, several statements will be executed before you can get the result on the terminal. We can define our own methods in Java. Let us discuss how to work with the methods in Java:

Creating Methods

To create Java methods, you should use the following syntax:

```
public static int method_Name(int x, int y) {
    // method body
}
```

Here is a description of the above syntax:

- **public static**- a modifier defining the accessibility of the method.

- **int**- the return type of the method.

- **method_Name**- the name of the method.

- **x, y**- formal parameters.

- **int x, int y**- a list of parameters.

The definition of a method comprises tthe method *header* and the *body*.

The following syntax best describes this:

```
modifier return_Type method_Name (Parameter List) {
   // method body
}
```

Here is a description of the above syntax:

- **modifier** – defines the method's access type, and it is optional.

- **returnType** – the method may return a value.

- **method_Name** – the name of the method. The method signature has the method name and parameter list.

- **Parameter List** – this is the list of method parameters, with the *type*, *order*, and *number* of parameters for the method. A method may have no parameters, making these optional.

- **method body** – this body defines what the method will do with the statements.

Here is an example of a Java method:

```java
/** a method to return the minimum of two numbers */
public static int minimumFunction(int p, int q) {
    int min;
    if (p > q)
        min = q;
    else
        min = p;

    return min;
}
```

In the above example, we have defined a method named *minimumFunction*. This function takes *two arguments* of an integer data type. The method should compare two integer values you pass to it and return the minimum one. Thus, we can define a method in Java.

Calling Methods

After defining a method, you can only use it by calling it. Note that depending on the definition of the method, it may or may not return a value. Once a program has called a method, the control of the program is shifted to the called method. The control will only be returned to the program under two conditions:

•   When the method has returned a value.

•   When the ending closing brace of the method has been reached.

The example given below will show how to define and call methods in Java:

```
public class MethodEXample {

    public static void main(String[] args) {
        int x = 10;
        int y = 13;
        int z = minimumFunction(x, y);
        System.out.println("The Minimum Value is " +
z);
    }

/** a method to return the minimum of two numbers */
    public static int minimumFunction(int p, int q) {
    int min;
    if (p > q)
       min = q;
    else
       min = p;

    return min;
    }
}
```

The code will print the following once executed:

The Minimum Value is 10

We have used the **minimumFunction** that checks and returns the minimum of two numbers. In the above example, we have passed to it the values **10** and **13**. It returned **10** since it is the minimum one.

The void Keyword

This is the keyword we used to define a method that should not return a value. Let us show this using an example:

```java
public class VoidKeywordExample {

    public static void main(String[] args) {
        totalPoints(71);
    }

    public static void totalPoints(double points) {
        if (points >= 62) {
            System.out.println("The government will sponsor your university fee");
        }else if (points >= 45) {
            System.out.println("You may have to sponsor your university fee");
        }else {
            System.out.println("You do not qualify for a chance in the university");
        }
    }
}
```

The code gives the output given below:

The government will sponsor your university fee

As you have noticed, we have not used the *return* keyword within the body of the method.

Call by Value

The method call is a way of invoking java functions. Java supports call-by-value. There is no call-by-reference in Java. When calling by-value, the original value isn't changed.

Example:

```
public class MethodCallExample{
    int p=20;

    void changeP(int p){
    p = p + 10;//changes to/in local variable
    }
    public static void main(String args[]){
      MethodCallExample mc=new MethodCallExample();

      System.out.println("The initial is "+mc.p);
      mc.changeP(50);
      System.out.println("the new value is "+mc.p);

    }
    }
```

The value won't change as shown in the following output:

> The initial is 20
> the new value is 20

When calling by-reference, the original value will change if changes are made to call method. If an object is passed in place of primitive value, the original value changes.

Example:

```
public class MethodCallExample{
    int p=20;
```

```
void changeP(MethodCallExample meth){
    meth.p=meth.p+50;//change to instance variable

}

public static void main(String args[]){
    MethodCallExample mc=new MethodCallExample();

    System.out.println("The initial value is
"+meth.val);
        meth.changeValue(meth);//passing the object
        System.out.println("The new value is
"+meth.val);

    }
}
```

The value has changed from **10** to **60**, after adding **50**. This is shown in the output given below:

> The initial value is 10
> The new value is 60

Abstract Methods

You may declare a method and then need its implementation to be done in child classes. The class can be marked as abstract in the parent class. Add abstract keyword before the method name. Abstract methods don't have a method body. You only add a **semicolon (;)** at its end.

Example:

```
public abstract class Worker {
    private String workerName;
```

58

```
private String workerAddress;
private int workerNumber;

public abstract double getPay();

}
```

Note that an **abstract** method must only be declared in the **abstract class**. The **getPay()** method above is abstract. We can have a class inheriting from the Worker class then implement the **getPay()** method in it:

```
public class Wage extends Worker {
    private double wake;

    public double getWage() {
        System.out.println("Getting wage for " +
getWorkerName());
        return wage/52;
    }
}
```

Method Overloading

This occurs when we have two or more methods with one name but different parameters. The difference in parameters can be in terms of number or type.

 Consider the example given below:

```
public class MethodOverloading {

    public static void main(String[] args) {
        int w = 11;
        int x = 6;
```

```
        double y = 7.3;
        double z = 9.4;
        int output1 = minimumFunction(w, x);

        // same function name but different parameters
        double output2 = minimumFunction(y, z);
        System.out.println("The minimum value is " +
output1);
        System.out.println("The minimum value is " +
output2);
    }

    // for integer
    public static int minimumFunction(int p, int q) {
        int min;
        if (p > q)
            min = q;
        else
            min = p;

        return min;
    }

    // for double
    public static double minimumFunction(double p,
double q) {
        double min;
        if (p > q)
            min = q;
        else
            min = p;

        return min;
    }
}
```

The code will give the following result after execution:

The minimum value is 6
The minimum value is 7.3

We have two functions with the same name: ***minimumFunction***. However, the first function takes ***integer*** arguments while the second one takes ***double*** arguments. We have then achieved method overloading.

Command-Line Arguments

Sometimes, it is necessary for you to pass information to the program during its execution. The best way to do this is by passing command-line arguments to the ***main()*** method.

Consider the line of code given below:

```
public static void main(String[] args) {
```

We referred to the above as the ***main()*** method and no Java program can be executed without this method. It can also be written as follows:

```
public static void main(String args[]) {
```

The [] denotes an array and we can pass arguments to it. Note that these arguments will begin from index **0**.

Consider the example given below:

```
public class CommandLineArguments {

    public static void main(String args[]) {
        for(int p = 0; p<args.length; p++) {
```

```
            System.out.println("args[" + p + "]: " +
args[p]);
        }
    }
}
```

Run the code from the command line. After compiling the code, pass the arguments to the terminal as showed below:

The this Keyword

The *this keyword* is used in Java to refer to the object of the current class, within a constructor or instance method. The keyword can be used for referencing the members of a class such as *variables, methods,* and *constructors*. It helps in differentiation between local variables and instance variables when they have similar names within a method or constructor.

The following example shows how this keyword can be used:

```
class Person {
    int age;
    Person(int age) {
        this.age = age;
    }
}
```

Let us show how we can use this keyword to access the various members of a class:

```java
public class This_Class {
    // an instance variable x
    int x = 10;

    This_Class() {
        System.out.println("Demonstrating the use of
this keyword in Java");
    }

    This_Class(int x) {
        // Invoke the default constructor
        this();

        // Assign the local variable num to instance
variable x
        this.x = x;
    }

    public void salute() {
        System.out.println("Welcome to Java
Programming");
    }

    public void print() {
        // Local variable x
        int x = 20;

        // Printing the local variable
        System.out.println("value of local variable num
is : "+x);

        // Print the instance variable
        System.out.println("The instance variable x has
a value of : "+this.x);

        // Invoke the salute method of a class
        this.salute();
    }

    public static void main(String[] args) {
        // Instantiate the class
        This_Class object1 = new This_Class();
```

```
    // Invoke the print method
    object1.print();

    // Pass a new value to variable x through a
parametrized constructor
    This_Class object2 = new This_Class(30);

    // Invoke the print method again
    object2.print();
  }
}
```

The code will return the following output once executed:

```
Demonstrating the use of this keyword in Java
value of local variable num is : 20
The instance variable x has a value of : 10
Welcome to Java Programming
Demonstrating the use of this keyword in Java
value of local variable num is : 20
The instance variable x has a value of : 30
Welcome to Java Programming
```

Variable Arguments

Java allowed passing a variable number of arguments to a method, but these must be of a similar type.

This can be done by declaring a parameter in the method as shown below:

```
type_Name... parameter_Name
```

When declaring the method, the type is specified then followed by an *ellipsis* (...). You can only specify one variable-length parameter in a method, and the parameter has to be the last parameter. If there are other regular parameters, they should precede it.

An example is given below:

```java
public class VariableArgumentsExample {

    public static void main(String args[]) {
        // Call a method with variable arguments
        showMax(11, 23, 87, 78.5, 43);
        showMax(new double[]{10, 22, 31});
    }

    public static void showMax( double... values) {
        if (values.length == 0) {
            System.out.println("No argument were
passed");
            return;
        }

        double output = values[0];

        for (int x = 1; x <  values.length; x++)
        if (values[x] >  output)
        output = values[x];
        System.out.println("The maximum value is " +
output);
    }
}
```

The code will return the following as the result:

```
The maximum value is 87.0
The maximum value is 31.0
```

Method Overriding

A subclass can override a method defined in the *parent* class if it was not declared with the *final* keyword. Overriding means overriding functionality of the existing method.

Example:

```java
class Mammal {
   public void run() {
      System.out.println("Mammals can run");
   }
}

class Cow extends Mammal {
   public void run() {
      System.out.println("Cows can run and eat");
   }
}

public class JavaTestOverriding {

   public static void main(String args[]) {
      Mammal ma = new Mammal ();    // Animal
reference and object
      Mammal mb = new Cow();    // Animal reference
but Cow object

      ma.run();    // to execute the method of Mammal
class
      mb.run();    // to execute the method of Cow
class

   }
}
```

The code returns the output given below:

```
Mammals can run
Cows can run and eat
```

Here, **mb** is a **_Mammal type_**, but it can use the method defined in **_Cow_** class.

Another Example:

We will take a bank example. Different banks offer different interest rates on loans:

```
class LendingInstitution{
    int getInterestRate(){
        return 0;

    }
    }

    class LendingInstitution1 extends
LendingInstitution{
    int getInterestRate(){
        return 10;

    }
    }

    class LendingInstitution2 extends
LendingInstitution{
    int getInterestRate(){
        return 11;

    }
    }
    class LendingInstitution3 extends
LendingInstitution{
    int getInterestRate(){
        return 14;

    }
    }

    public class TestLendingInstitution{
    public static void main(String args[]){
```

```
    LendingInstitution1 l1=new LendingInstitution1();
    LendingInstitution2 l2=new LendingInstitution2();
    LendingInstitution3 l3=new LendingInstitution3();
    System.out.println("LendingInstitution1 Interest
Rate: "+l1.getInterestRate());
    System.out.println("LendingInstitution1 Interest
Rate: "+l2.getInterestRate());
    System.out.println("LendingInstitution1 Interest
Rate: "+l3.getInterestRate());
    }
    }
```

The code should give the result given below:

```
LendingInstitution1 Interest Rate: 10
LendingInstitution1 Interest Rate: 11
LendingInstitution1 Interest Rate: 14
```

The method *getInterestRate()* has been used differently for different classes.

We can use the *"super"* keyword to access a method overridden from the *super* class.

Example:

```
class Mammals {
    public void run() {
        System.out.println("Mammals can run");
    }
}

class Cow extends Mammals {
    public void run() {
        super.run();    // to invoke method in super
class
        System.out.println("Cows can run and eat");
    }
}
```

```
public class TestCow {

    public static void main(String args[]) {
        Mammals mm = new Cow();    // mammal reference
but Cow object
        mm.run();    // to execute method in Cow class
    }
}
```

The code prints the output is given below:

```
Mammals can run
Cows can run and eat
```

Recursive Functions in Java

Recursion is a process by which a method calls itself repeatedly. The method becomes a *recursive* method. With recursive methods, a code will be compact but complicated for understanding.

Recursion syntax:

```
returntype method(){
//code to run
method();//call same method
}
```

Example:

```
public class JavaRecursionExample {
static void helloMethod(){
System.out.println("Hello there");
helloMethod();
}
```

```
public static void main(String[] args) {
helloMethod();
}
}
```

If you run the above code, it will keep on printing the ***Hello there*** text. The method ***helloMethod()*** will call itself infinite times because we have not specified the number of times that the method should call itself. The implementation for a method to call itself finite times may be implemented in this way:

```
public class JavaRecursionExample2 {
    static int times=0;
    static void helloMethod(){
    times++;
    if(times<=10){
    System.out.println("Hello there "+times);
    helloMethod();
    }
    }
    public static void main(String[] args) {
    helloMethod();
    }
    }
```

The code returns the following output:

```
C:\Users\admin>javac JavaRecursionExample2.java

C:\Users\admin>java JavaRecursionExample2
Hello there 1
Hello there 2
Hello there 3
Hello there 4
Hello there 5
Hello there 6
Hello there 7
Hello there 8
Hello there 9
Hello there 10

C:\Users\admin>
```

We are increasing the value of ***times*** variable until it reaches **10**.

Note **<=10** means **10** is included. That is why the method prints up to the **10th time**. With recursion, we can get the factorial of a number.

Let us show this with an example:

```java
public class JavaRecursionExample3 {
      static int numberFactorial(int nm){
          if (nm == 1)
            return 1;
          else
            return(nm * numberFactorial(nm-1));
      }

   public static void main(String[] args) {
   System.out.println("The result of 10 factorial
is: "+numberFactorial(10));
   }
   }
```

The code will return the following output:

```
The result of 10 factorial is: 3628800
```

For the factorial, a number is multiplied by its preceding numbers except **0**.

With recursion, we may get **Fibonacci** for number.

Example:

```java
public class JavaRecursionExample4 {
      static int x=0,y=1,z=0;
       static void showFib(int times){
          if(times>0){
               z = x + y;
               x = y;
               y = z;
```

```
            System.out.print(" "+z);
            showFib(times-1);
       }
    }

public static void main(String[] args) {
    int times=18;
       System.out.print(x+" "+y);//print 0, 1
       showFib(times-2);//2 numbers already
printed
    }
}
```

The code will return the result given below:

```
0 1 1 2 3 5 8 13 21 34 55 89 144 233 377 610 987 1597
```

Note that the **Fibonacci** of a number is the sum of two of its previous numbers. In the above example, we have done the recursion for **18** times.

10-Inheritance in Java

In inheritance, an object gains the behaviors and properties of another object. The object gaining the behaviors and the properties becomes the *child*, while the object from which they are inherited is the *parent*. They can also be referred to as *subclass* and *superclass*, respectively. Inheritance makes information manageable in a hierarchical order. The methods that had been defined in the superclass can be reused in the subclass without defining them again.

To Inherit from a parent class, we use the extends keyword. Inheritance is done using the syntax given below:

```
class Child-class-name extends Parent-class-name
{
    // fields  and methods
}
```

The *extends* keyword is an indication that we are creating some new class from the existing class.

Example:

```
class Employee{
     float employee_salary=60000;

    }
    public class Developer extends Employee{
     int commision=20000;
     public static void main(String args[]){
        Developer d=new Developer();
        System.out.println("developer salary
is:"+d.employee_salary);
        System.out.println("Commision for Developer
is:"+d.commision);
    }
    }
```

The will return the following when executed:

```
developer salary is:60000.0
Commision for Developer is:20000
```

We first created a class named *Employee*. This forms the *parent* class for an example. We have then created the class named *Developer* which extends the *Employee class*. The Developer class becomes the *child* class. We have created an instance/object of the Developer class and given it the name *d*. By using this instance; we could access a variable that was defined in the *parent* class.

There are different types of inheritance in Java. Let us discuss them:

Single Inheritance

Here, a *single* class inherits from another class. The *Worker* and *DBA* classes given previously are an example of this.

Example:

```
class Mammal{
void run(){
    System.out.println("Running...");
        }
}
class Cow extends Mammal{
void moow(){System.out.println("Moowing...");}
}
public class JavaInheritance{
public static void main(String args[]){
Cow cw=new Cow();
cw.moow();
cw.run();
    }
}
```

The code will return the following result after execution:

```
Moowing...
Running...
```

In the above example, the *run()* method has been defined in the *Mammal* class while the *moow()* method has been defined in *Cow* class which extends the *Mammal* class. In the *JavaInheritance* class, we have created an instance of *Cow* class and named it **cw**. We have then used this instance to access the two methods that have been defined in two different classes.

Multilevel Inheritance

This type of inheritance occurs when **class B** inherits from **class A**, while **class C** inherits from **class B**.

Here is an example:

```java
class Mammal{
    void run(){
        System.out.println("Running...");

    }
    }
    class Cow extends Mammal{
    void moow(){
        System.out.println("Moowing...");

    }
    }
    class BabyCow extends Cow{
    void eat(){
        System.out.println("Eating...");}
    }
    public class JavaInheritanceTest2{
    public static void main(String args[]){
    BabyCow bc=new BabyCow();
    bc.moow();
    bc.eat();
    bc.run();
    }
}
```

The code will return the result given below:

```
Moowing...
Eating...
Running...
```

The *run()* method has been defined in the *Mammal* class. The *moow()* method is defined in the ***Cow*** class which extends the ***Mammal*** class. The *eat()* method has been defined in the ***BabyCow*** class which extends the ***Cow*** class. In the ***InheritanceTest2*** class, we have created an instance of ***BabyCow*** class named *bc*. This instance has then been used to access various properties or methods. We can use the instance of ***BabyCow*** class to access methods defined in the ***Cow*** and ***Mammal*** classes. The methods in various classes can be seen as their properties.

Hierarchical Inheritance

This type of inheritance can be demonstrated with this example:

```
class Mammal{
    void run(){
        System.out.println("Running...");

    }
}
    class Cow extends Mammal{
    void moow(){
        System.out.println("Moowing...");

    }
}
    class Goat extends Mammal{
    void meew(){
        System.out.println("Meewing...");

    }
}
  public class JavaInheritanceTest{
  public static void main(String args[]){
  Goat gt=new Goat();
  gt.meew();
  gt.run();
  //gt.moow(); will give an Error
```

```
    }
  }
```

After creating an instance of **Goat** class in the **InheritanceTest** class, we canto inherit the properties defined in the **Mammal** class since the **Goat** class inherits from **Mammal** class. However, we cannot to access the properties defined in the **Cow** class since the **Goat** class does not inherit from the **Cow** class. If we attempt to do that, for example, run the **gt.moow();** statement, we will get an error.

Some programming languages support multiple inheritance, in which a single class inherits from the others classes. Java doesn't support that, and the only possibility that let us get to this is by creating an interface, and then use the implements on the interface. Suppose that we have an interface named **Interface1**, and then we can create a class named **Class2** that extends from **Class1** and implements the interface **Interface1**:

```
public class Class2 extends Class1 implements
Interface1{
}
```

That is the closest way by where we can get to the multiple inheritance feature in Java. For the class, we keyword **"extends"**, but this cannot be used for an interface. Instead, we use keyword implements. By this way, we can inherit the features of an interface. Inheritance helps in the reuse of existing properties and methods.

Invoking Superclass Constructor

For a class that is inheriting properties from another class, the child class automatically inherits the default constructor of the superclass. However, when you need to call a parameterized constructor of a superclass, you are required to use *super* keyword with the syntax given below:

```
super(values);
```

The following example demonstrates this:

```
class MySuperclass {
    int x;

    MySuperclass(int x) {
        this.x = x;
    }

    public void getX() {
        System.out.println("The value of x in super
class is: " +x);
    }
}

public class MySubclass extends MySuperclass {
    MySubclass(int x) {
        super(x);
    }

    public static void main(String argd[]) {
        MySubclass sb = new MySubclass(32);
        sb.getX();
    }
}
```

The code will give the following output when executed:

```
The value of x in super class is: 32
```

In the example given above, we demonstrated how we can use the *super* keyword to accesses a parameterized constructor defined in the *superclass*. The program has both a *parent* class and a *child* class, with the *superclass* having a parameterized constructor that takes in an *integer* value. We have then used the *super* keyword for the purpose of accessing this constructor.

The instance of Keyword

This keyword can be used for checking when an object is an instance of another object. Let us show this with an example:

```java
interface Mammal{}
class Cow implements Mammal{}

public class BabyCow extends Cow {

    public static void main(String args[]) {
        Cow c = new Cow();
        BabyCow bc = new BabyCow();

        System.out.println(c instanceof Mammal);
        System.out.println(bc instanceof Cow);
        System.out.println(bc instanceof Mammal);
    }
}
```

The code should return the following result:

```
true
true
true
```

This screenshot shows that our tests were true. It means that *Cow* is an instance of *Mammal*, *BabyCow* is an instance of *Cow* and *BabyCow* is an instance of *Mammal*.

11-Abstraction in Java

Abstraction is a feature that makes a developer present to the user, only what is necessary and hides the rest. The developer must differentiate what is necesary to be presented to the users from what is not. When you send an email, for example, you need to type the content, attach documents and press the *"Send"* button, without knowing what happens behind the scenes. Also, when you drive a car, you press the accelerator and you see the speed increasing, and when you press the brakes your car stops. You don't know what happens in the background. This is the abstraction we will talk about, in this chapter.

With abstraction, users aren't aware of the implementation details. The developer hides them. The user gets only the functionality of the app. Thus, the user gets information on what app does rather than how it's done. An *abstract* class has the *abstract* keyword. If any class has an abstract method, it must be recognized as an *abstract*. The *abstract* class must also be inherited from some other abstract class.

Example:

```
abstract class Student {
 abstract void register();
}

public class John extends Student {
 void register() {
  System.out.println("John is going for
registration");
 }

 public static void main(String argu[]) {
  Student st = new John();
  st.register();
  System.out.println("Done");
 }
 }
```

The code returns the result given below upon execution:

```
John is going for registration
Done
```

It is unnecessary for an *abstract* class to have *abstract* methods in it. You can't instantiate an *abstract* class. That is why we instantiated *John* class as it has inherited a method from an abstract class.

Example:

```java
public abstract class Worker {
    private String name;
    private String workerAddress;
    private int number;

    public Worker(String name, String workerAddress,
int number) {
        System.out.println("Worker Construction");
        this.name = name;
        this.workerAddress = workerAddress;
        this.number = number;
    }

    public double getWorkerSalary() {
        System.out.println("Inside getWorkerSalary ");
        return 0.00;
    }

    public void checkMail() {
        System.out.println("Sending check to " +
this.name + " " + this.workerAddress);
    }

    public String toString() {
        return name + " " + workerAddress + " " +
number;
    }

    public String getWorkerName() {
        return name;
    }

    public String getWorkerAddress() {
        return workerAddress;
    }

    public void setWorkerAddress(String
newWorkerAddress) {
        workerAddress = newWorkerAddress;
    }

    public int getWorkerNumber() {
        return number;
    }
}
```

The *class Worker* is like other Java classes except for the use of the *abstract* keyword. Attempt to instantiate it:

```java
public class InstantiateAbstract {

    public static void main(String [] args) {
        /* This will generate error */
        Worker wk = new Worker("Tony S.", "Texas, USA",
35);
        System.out.println("\n Calling checkMail with
Worker reference");
        wk.checkMail();
    }
}
```

The properties of the *Worker* class must be inherited rather than instantiating the class.

Example:

```java
public class Wage extends Worker {
    private double wage;    // Annual salary

    public Wage(String name, String workerAddress, int
number, double wage) {
        super(name, workerAddress, number);
        setWage(wage);
    }

    public void checkMail() {
        System.out.println("In checkMail for Wage class
");
        System.out.println("Sending check to " +
getWorkerName() + " with wage " + wage);
    }

    public double getWage() {
        return wage;
    }

    public void setWage(double newWage) {
        if(newWage >= 0.0) {
```

```
            wage = newWage;
        }
    }

    public double getWorkerPay() {
        System.out.println("Getting wage for " +
getWorkerName());
        return wage/52;
    }
}
```

The *Worker* class cannot be instantiated, but *Wage* class can be instantiated and then we can use its instance to access all fields and methods of *Worker* class.

Example:

```
public class AbstractInsta {

    public static void main(String [] args) {
        Wage w = new Wage("Don Lilly", "New York, USA",
4, 3400.00);
        Worker wk = new Wage("Lopez Terez",
"Washington, USA", 3, 3800.00);
        System.out.println("Calling checkMail via Wage
reference");
        w.checkMail();
        System.out.println("\n Calling checkMail via
Worker reference");
        wk.checkMail();
    }
}
```

To run the above codes, you must create files in different files compile and execute the *last* class.

Then, you will get the results. This is showed below:

```
C:\Users\admin>javac Worker.java

C:\Users\admin>javac Wage.java

C:\Users\admin>javac AbstractInsta.java

C:\Users\admin>java AbstractInsta
Worker Construction
Worker Construction
Calling checkMail via Wage reference
In checkMail for Wage class
Sending check to Don Lilly with wage 3400.0

 Calling checkMail via Worker reference
In checkMail for Wage class
Sending check to Lopez Terez with wage 3800.0

C:\Users\admin>
```

12-Encapsulation

Encapsulation is a feature of object-oriented programming that helps in **grouping data** and **methods** together. The data are the variables while methods are the codes that let us act on the data. With encapsulation, class variables can be hidden from other classes and the access to them may only be possible via methods of the class. Encapsulation works as a ***Data Hiding***. It's achieved by setting *class* variables as ***private***. The *"setter"* and *"getter"* methods for the variables should be set as public and be used to change the value of the variables.

Example:

```
public class Workers{
private String name;

public String getWorkerName(){
return name;
}
public void setWorkerName(String name){
this.name=name;
```

```
}
}
```
You can add a **new** file to same package with **this** code:
```
public class TestWorkers {
public static void main(String[] args){
Workers wk=new Workers();
wk.setWorkerName("Joel");
System.out.println(wk.getWorkerName());
}
}
```

The code gives the following output:

```
C:\Users\admin>javac Workers.java

C:\Users\admin>javac TestWorkers.java

C:\Users\admin>java TestWorkers
Joel

C:\Users\admin>
```

The variable name was marked as *private* in *Workers* class. The methods *setWorkerName()* and get*WorkerName()* were set as public in *Workers* class. We have instantiated *Students* class in *TestWorkers* class, then we have used this instance to access its variable and methods.

Another example:

```
public class MyClass {
    private String personName;
    private String personID;
    private int personAge;

    public int getAge() {
        return personAge;
    }
```

```
public String getName() {
    return personName;
}

public String getID() {
    return personID;
}

public void setAge( int newPersonAge) {
    personAge = newPersonAge;
}

public void setName(String newPersonName) {
    personName = newPersonName;
}

public void setID( String newPersonID) {
    personID = newPersonID;
}
}
```

Any class that needs of accessing private variables must use public methods: the *setters* and *getters*.

We access using methode given below:

```
public class MyClassTest extends MyClass{

    public static void main(String args[]) {
        MyClassTest mct = new MyClassTest();
        mct.setName("Joel");
        mct.setAge(32);
        mct.setID("4458972");

        System.out.print("Name : " + mct.getName() + "
Age : " + mct.getAge());
    }
}
```

You should write the two codes in two separate files. Upon

execution, you should get the following result:

```
C:\Users\admin>javac MyClass.java

C:\Users\admin>javac MyClassTest.java

C:\Users\admin>java MyClassTest
Name : Joel Age : 32
C:\Users\admin>
```

13-Interfaces

An interface is a *blueprint* for a class. It comes with both *abstract* methods and *static* constants. The Interface provides a mechanism for achieving abstraction. An interface must only have abstract methods rather than the method body. It's very important for achieving multiple inheritances. It's similar to a class, but with abstract methods only. Any class must implement an interface to use its methods. Other than *abstract* methods, it may have *constants*, *static* methods, *default* methods, *nested* types, etc.

An interface has methods that can be implemented by classes. To implement interface methods, a *class* must be abstract. Otherwise, all interface methods must be defined in the class. An interface can't be instantiated. It also can't have constructors. All its fields must be final or static, not instance fields.

To set one, we use the interface keyword.

Here is the Syntax:

```
interface <interfaceName>{
          //constant fields
    // abstract methods
}
```

An interface is an implicit abstract; hence we don't add abstract keyword when declaring it. The methods are implicitly abstract; hence we don't use abstract keyword when declaring them. They are implicitly public.

Example:

```
interface Mammal {
    public void run();
    public void eat();
}
```

An interface may be implemented using the class:

```
interface Mammal {
    public void run();
    public void eat();
}


public class Cow implements Mammal{
    public void run(){
      System.out.println("Interface Method run already
Implemented");
  }
  public void eat(){
      System.out.println("Interface Method eat already
Implemented");
  }
   public static void main(String args[]){
     Mammal mm = new Cow();
     mm.run();
     mm.eat();
  }
```

}

The code should return the following result after execution:

```
Interface Method run already Implemented
Interface Method eat already Implemented
```

We created interface *Mammal* which has been implemented by *Cow* class. Its *run()* and *eat()* methods have been used in *Cow* class.

For two interfaces, one interface may extend another one via the extends keyword. The *sub-interface* (child) will inherit methods of *super-interface* (parent).

Example:

```
public interface Toyotas {
    public void setCarPrice(String carPrice);
    public void setCC(String cc);
}


public interface Harrier extends Toyotas {
    public void maximumMileage(int miles);
    public void seats(int seats);
    public void kilometersPerLiter(int kms);
}


public interface Prado extends Toyotas {
    public void interiorSpace();
    public void carLength();
    public void setCarPrice(String carPrice);
    public void setCC(String cc);
}
```

We defined *Toyotas* interface. The others, *Harrier* and *Prado* are extending the *Toyotas* interface. The interface *Prado* has four methods, but two of these have been inherited from Toyotas interface. You may inherit from several interfaces by use of (,) to separate them.

Example:

```
public interface Harrier extends Toyotas, Cars
```

Java doesn't support multiple inheritances, however, we may achieve it via interfaces.

Here is another interface example:

```
interface ObjectInterface{
void drawObject();
static int cubeObject(int ab){return ab*ab*ab;}
}
class Cuboid implements ObjectInterface{
public void drawObject(){
System.out.println("drawing cuboid");
}
}
public class InterfaceTest{
public static void main(String args[]){
ObjectInterface ob=new Cuboid();
ob.drawObject();
System.out.println(ObjectInterface.cubeObject(3));
}
}
```

A *nested* interface is the one we can add inside another interface.

Example:

```
interface Message{
 void printMessage();
 interface ShortMessage{
```

```
    void message();
 }
}
```

The *ShortMessage* interface has been defined inside the *Message* interface, making it a *nested* interface.

14-Packages

Packages are essentials for grouping related interfaces and classes together. The grouping is determined by functionality. With packages, we can group classes and find the ones we need easily to avoid conflicts. It is recommended that you create a package and then use it to group related *classes*, *interfaces,* etc. With packages, it's easy to access variables and methods defined in classes and interfaces in the same package.

A Java package can be user-defined or built-in. Examples of built-in Java packages include **lang**, **awt**, **java**, **javax**, **net**, **io**, **swing**, **util**, **sql,** and others. To use these packages, use the import statement to be made available in your class. To create packages, use package keyword then package name.

Example:

```java
package firstpackage;
public class MyPackage{
  public static void main(String args[]){
    System.out.println("My first package");
```

```
        }
}
```

Execution of the above codes will return the following output:

```
My first package
```

The *package definition* statement is always with a semicolon (;). When we create packages, we should use *lowercase* letters for the name to avoid conflicting with the *interface/class* names.

Another Example:

```java
package animal;

interface Mammals {
    public void run();
    public void eat();
}
```

We have created a package named *animal* with an interface named *Mammals*. We can now implement the interface in package *animal*:

```java
package animal;

public class Cow implements Mammals {

    public void run() {
        System.out.println("Cows run");
    }

    public void eat() {
        System.out.println("Cows eat");
    }
```

```
public int legCount() {
   return 0;
}

public static void main(String args[]) {
   Cow c = new Cow();
   c.run();
   c.eat();
}
}
```

The code will return the following result:

```
Cows run
Cows eat
```

If we do not use a package, the two may be combined into one:

```
interface Mammals {
   public void run();
   public void eat();
}


public class Cow implements Mammals {

   public void run() {
      System.out.println("Cows run");
   }

   public void eat() {
      System.out.println("Cows eat");
   }

   public int legCount() {
      return 0;
   }

   public static void main(String args[]) {
      Cow c = new Cow();
      c.run();
```

```
        c.eat();
    }
}
```

Import Keyword

You can access packages outside a certain package. Using the *import* keyword is one of the possibilities to do it. To access a class in the same package, it unnecessary for a package to be used. After importing class using the ***packagename.classname*** syntax, only methods in imported class will be accessible.

Example:

```
package hellopackage;
public class HelloClass{
    public void messsage(){
System.out.println("Hello there!");
}
}
```

We have a class named ***"HelloClass"*** defined in a package named ***"hellopackage"*** and we save it in the file ***HelloClass.java***. We have this class:

```
package studentspackage;

  class HelloStudentsClass{
    public static void main(String args[]){
    HelloClass hello = new HelloClass();
     hello.message();
    }
  }
```

The second program will generate an error once executed. We have instantiated the class ***HelloClass*** to get the instance ***hello***. We have used the instance to access *message()* method defined in *HelloClass*. Note that they are not in a single package. This will generate an error. The reason is we instantiate a class not in the same package as the current one. We have to import the class, *HelloClass* from package *hellopackage*. We use *packagename.classname* syntax at the top of the class:

```
package studentspackage1;
import hellopackage.HelloClass;

 class HelloStudentsClass{
   public static void main(String args[]){
   HelloClass hello = new HelloClass();
    hello.message();
   }
 }
```

A name for *package* and *class* is useful to avoid an error. With this methode, we do not need to use the import keyword since the name will direct us to the package and class, and then the method will be accessible from there.

Example:

```
package hellopackage;
public class HelloClass{
   public void messsage(){
System.out.println("Hello there!");
}
}
```

To use the *message()* method in a class in another package, we can do it as follows:

```
package studentspacks;

 class HelloStudentsClass{
```

```
   public static void main(String args[]){
    hellopackage.HelloClass hello = new
hellopackage.HelloClass();
     hello.message();
    }
  }
```

Consider this line:

```
hellopackage.HelloClass hello = new
hellopackage.HelloClass();
```

The *hellopackage.HelloClass* helps us access *HelloClass* class in a package named *hellopackage*. After that, we can access the *message()* method defined in the class. Note that you access methods and variables in that class only, not in other classes of the package.

Another example

```
package armory;
interface guns {
 public void pistol();

}
```

The *guns* interface is in *armory* interface. We can implement the interface in the similar package:

```
package armory;
public class ceska implements guns {
 public void bullets() {
  System.out.println("Ceska has bullets");
 }
 public void pistol() {
  System.out.println("It has 5 bullets");
 }
```

```
public int owner() {
 return 0;
}
public static void main(String args[]) {
 ceska cs = new ceska();
 cs.bullets();

}
}
```

15-Java Applets

Applets are Java programs that run on web browsers. An applet may act as a fully functional app since it comes with a full Java API. The applet class extends *java.applet.Applet*. Applets don't have the main method, hence they don't invoke *main()*. They are instead embedded on HTML pages. After an HTML page with an applet is opened, its code is downloaded to the local machine. The JVM (Java Virtual Machine) is mandatory for you to view applets.

Applets are processed on the client side; hence they give users a quick response compared to other apps. Applets offer good security.

Applets' Lifecycle

Applets go through these steps:

1. **Initialization**- the *init()* method initializes applets.

2. **Starting**- the *start()* method starts applets.

3. **Painting**- done after calling *paint()* method.

4. **Stopping**- we invoke *stop()* method to stop an applet.

5. **Destroying**- the applet is destroyed by invoking *destroy()* method.

Applets are viewed by HTML.

Example:

Create a new file in text editor with name *FirstApplet.java.* and add this code to it:

```java
import java.awt.Graphics;
import java.applet.Applet;
public class FirstApplet extends Applet{

public void paint(Graphics gc){
gc.drawString("Our First Applet!",150,150);
 }
}
```

Create new file in editor named mycode.html. Add this code to it:

```html
<html>
<body>
<applet code="FirstApplet.class" width="320"
height="320">
</applet>
</body>
</html>
```

First, we have Java code in which we added code regarding what our applet should do. The class is named MyApplet. Consider this:

```java
gc.drawString("Our First Applet!",150,150);
```

We are drawing the *"Our First Applet!* Text at points **150, 150** of the applet window. Note the two libraries added via import statement: **Graphics** and **Applet libraries**. The *paint()* method is defined in *Graphics* library. If we don't import it, an error will be generated since Java compiler won't understand what we mean. We have HTML code in file *mycode.html*. In this, we created a window on which to draw text.

Note how we have linked HTML code and Java code:

```
<applet code="FirstApplet.class" width="320"
height="320">
```

We linked to *FirstApplet.class* rather than *FirstApplet.java*. This means Java code should compile first to give the *.class* file, then HTML code will recognize it.

Open the OS terminal, navigate to the location of the files. Run this command to compile Java code:

```
javac FirstApplet.java
```

This will generate *FirstApplet.class* file. We can use the *appletviewer* for our applet viewing. Run this command on the console:

```
appletviewer mycode.html
```

A window should popup with the text *OurFirstApplet*!. That is the Applet.

```
C:\Users\admin>javac FirstApplet.java

C:\Users\admin>appletviewer mycode.html
```

Change the point where the text is drawn by altering the coordinates. It will change the location on the window.

Try this and see the shapes generated:

Create file *MyPaint.java* with this code:

```java
import java.applet.Applet;
import java.awt.*;
public class Mypaint extends Applet
{
public void paint(Graphics gc){
gc.drawOval(130, 40, 60, 50);

gc.drawOval(120, 60, 10, 15);
gc.drawOval(190, 60, 10, 15);

gc.drawOval(160, 50, 10, 10);
gc.drawOval(140, 50, 10, 10);
gc.drawOval(150, 70, 15, 10);
gc.drawRect(145, 90, 30, 30);
```

```
gc.drawRect(120, 120, 80, 120);
gc.drawRect(130, 240, 20, 120 );
gc.drawRect(170, 240, 20, 120);

gc.drawRect(130, 360, 30, 20);
gc.drawRect(170, 360, 30, 20);

gc.drawLine(200,160,240,240);
gc.drawLine(240,240, 280,160);

gc.drawRect(280, 130, 120, 30);
gc.setColor (Color.blue);
gc.fillRect (280, 130, 120, 30);

gc.drawRect(280, 160, 120, 30);
gc.setColor (Color.yellow);
gc.fillRect (280, 160, 120, 30);

gc.drawRect(280, 190, 120, 30);
gc.setColor (Color.red);
gc.fillRect (280, 190, 120, 30);

}
}
```

Create new file **mycode2.html** with this code:

```
<HTML>
<TITLE>Hellow World</TITLE>
<HEAD>Our Hello Applet</HEAD>
<Applet code="Mypaint.class" width=500 height=500>
</Applet>
</html>
```

Compile **MyPaint.java**, then run **mycode2.html**. This is demonstrated below:

```
javac MyPaint.java
appletviewer mycode2.html
```

This should give you the following output:

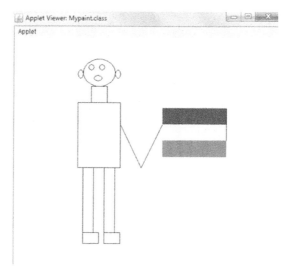

Graphics library comes with functions/methods that can draw numerous shapes. To draw an oval shape, call **drawOval()** method. Pass 4 parameters to it, which are the points to be touched by edges of the oval. To draw a rectangle, call **drawRect()** method and pass 4 coordinates to it which specify its corners. The **drawLine()** method helps one draw a line. The **setColor()** method helps in setting object color.

Example 3:

Write this code in **OurPaintClass.java** file:

```java
import java.applet.Applet;
import java.awt.*;
public class OurPaintClass extends Applet
{
public void paint(Graphics g){

g.drawRect(120, 120, 160, 120);
g.drawLine(120, 120, 440, 365);

}
}
```

Its HTML code should be as follows:

```
<HTML>
<TITLE>Hello World</TITLE>
<HEAD>Our Hello Applet</HEAD>
<Applet code="OurPaintClass.class" width=500
height=500>
</Applet>
</html>
```

Compile the OurPaintClass.java class then run OurPaint.html code with appletviewer.

You will get the result given below:

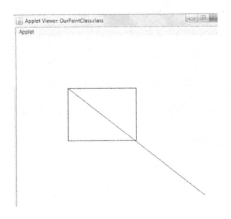

Displaying Images

Images can be displayed on applets as applets are popular in animations and games. The class java.awt.Graphics has a *drawImage()* method for image display. The method *getImage()*

returns an image object. The method ***getCodeBase()*** returns base URL. The ***getDocumentBase()*** image returns document URL in which applet has been embedded.

Example:

```java
import java.awt.*;
import java.applet.*;
public class ImageDisplay extends Applet {

  Image img;

  public void init(){
    img =
getImage(getDocumentBase(),"imagename.png");
  }

  public void paint(Graphics gc) {
    gc.drawImage(img, 30,30, this);
  }

}
```

The ***drawImage()*** method displays the image. Its **4th** parameter is an object for ***ImageObserver***. Save the code in a file named ***ImageDisplay.java***. Add this code to a file named ***imagedisplay.html***:

```html
<html>
<body>
<applet code="ImageDisplay.class" width="350"
height="350">
</applet>
</body>
</html>
```

Compile Java class via command javac ***ImageDisplay.java***, then invoke the imagedisplay.html file via ***appletviewer***. If you specified a correct image in the same directory with these files, it will be shown on the window.

Applet Animations

Since applets are common in games, images should be moved. Example:

Create file AnimationExample.java. Add this code:

```java
import java.applet.*;
    import java.awt.*;
    public class AnimationExample extends Applet {

    Image img;

    public void init() {
       img =getImage(getDocumentBase(),"car.gif");
    }

    public void paint(Graphics gc) {
       for(int p=0;p<500;p++){
          gc.drawImage(img, p,30, this);

          try{
             Thread.sleep(100);

          }
          catch(Exception ex){

          }
       }
    }
}
```

The method *drawImage()* helps us display an image. Create new file named ***animation.html***. and add this code:

```html
<html>
```

```
<body>
<applet code="AnimationExample.class" width="350"
height="300">
</applet>
</body>
</html>
```

Compile the *.java* class then run the *.html* file. Ensure the correct image is specified in the *.java* class and keep it in the same directory as the files. It will move after running the code.

Events on Applets

Events may be added on applets. Here, we add an event for applet to display a message after clicking button:

Create file *AppletEvent.java* then add this code:

```
import java.applet.*;
import java.awt.event.*;
import java.awt.*;
public class AppletEventExample extends Applet
implements ActionListener{
    Button btn;
    TextField txt;

    public void init(){
    txt=new TextField();
    txt.setBounds(30,40,150,20);

    btn=new Button("Click");
    btn.setBounds(80,150,60,50);

    add(btn);
add(txt);
    btn.addActionListener(this);

    setLayout(null);
```

```
    }

    public void actionPerformed(ActionEvent ev){
      txt.setText("Text on Applet");
    }
  }
```

Note the applet class implements an interface named *ActionListener*. This has methods for listening to action events and responding appropriately. New classes have been introduced: *Button* and *Textfield* classes. We created instances of these classes, that is, *btn* and *txt* respectively to get a button and a *textfield*. The *text* Click was added to the button, and *setBounds()* method is for setting the bounds for the two elements. Consider this:

```
btn.addActionListener(this);
```

The command adds action listener event to our button, the button will wait or listen to be clicked. After the click, the action specified in the *actionPerformed()* method will be performed.

Create new file *myapplet.html* then add this:

```
<html>
    <body>
    <applet code="AppletEventExample.class"
width="350" height="350">
    </applet>
    </body>
    </html>
```

Compile your Java code via command *javac AppletEventExample.java*, then invoke the **.html** file via

appletviewer myapplet.html. The following applet window will pop up:

Click the **"Click"** button. A new message will be added to ***textfield*** as shown below:

Applet Parameters

Information on HTML file may be used as a parameter to the applet. The parameters may be acquired via the ***getParameter()***

method of Applet class. Example:

Create a new file, *AppletParameters.java*. Add this code:

```
import java.awt.Graphics;
    import java.applet.Applet;

    public class AppletParametersExample extends
Applet{
    public void paint(Graphics g){
    String st=getParameter("message");
    g.drawString(st,50, 50);
    }
    }
```

Create new file for HTML code, *appletcode.html*:

```
<html>
<body>
<applet code="AppletParameters.class" width="350"
height="350">
<param name="message" value="Applet Parameters">
</applet>
</body>
</html>
```

In the above HTML code, the value for *param name* should much the value of the argument passed to *getParameter()* method in Java class.

Now, compile your Java code via javac *AppletParametersExample.java* command. The *AppletParametersExample.class* file will be generated. Invoke the html code via *appletviewer appletcode.html*.

You should then get the window given below:

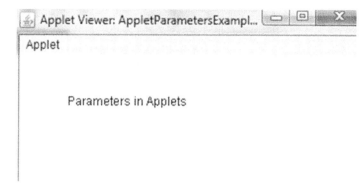

This text was specified in the value attribute of *param name* in HTML code.

16-Java Input/ Output

The *java.io* package comes with many classes we can use to perform *input/output* tasks. The *input/output* concept in Java is implemented by the use of streams. The stream is provided with the java.io package and it supports different types of data including localized *variables*, *object*, *primitives,* etc.

A stream is simply a sequence of data. There are two types of Streams:

- **InPutStream** – used for reading data from the source.

- **OutPutStream** –used for writing data to the destination.

Byte Streams

Java streams are made up of bytes. The Java byte streams perform *input/output* operations of **8-bit bytes**. There are several classes that are related to the byte streams, but the common ones are *FileInputStream* and *FileOutputStream*. Let us use an example which demonstrates how we can use these two classes:

```java
import java.io.*;
public class CopyingFiles {

    public static void main(String args[]) throws
IOException {
        FileInputStream inp = null;
        FileOutputStream outp = null;

        try {
            inp = new FileInputStream("colleagues.txt");
            outp = new FileOutputStream("output.txt");

            int ch;
            while ((ch = inp.read()) != -1) {
                outp.write(ch);
            }
        }finally {
            if (inp != null) {
                inp.close();
            }
            if (outp != null) {
                outp.close();
            }
        }
    }
}
```

The code will read the contents of the file *colleagues.txt* and copy them into a new file named *output.txt*. Note that the latter will be created automatically, and the contents copied into it.

Character Streams

Character Streams are used for performing *input* and *output* operations of **16-bit Unicode**. There are many classes that are associated with character streams. The most popular are the *FileReader* and *FileWriter*. Internally, the *FileReader* uses the *FileInputStream* while *FileWriter* uses *FileOutputStream*, but the major difference between them is that the *FileReader* reads two bytes each time while *FileWriter* writes two bytes each time. Let us use these two classes to rewrite our previous example:

```java
import java.io.*;
public class CopyingFiles {

    public static void main(String args[]) throws
IOException {
        FileReader inp = null;
        FileWriter outp = null;

        try {
            inp = new FileReader("colleagues.txt");
            outp = new FileWriter("output.txt");

            int ch;
            while ((ch = inp.read()) != -1) {
                outp.write(ch);
            }
        }finally {
            if (inp != null) {
                inp.close();
            }
            if (outp != null) {
                outp.close();
            }
        }
    }
}
```

When you compile and run the code, it will copy the contents of the file ***colleagues.txt*** into a new file named ***output.txt.***

Standard Streams

In each programming language, a way is provided through which a user can enter input through the keyboard and the input will be displayed on the computer screen. We have three standard streams we can use for this purpose:

• **Standard Input** − used for feeding data to the user's program with the keyboard and used as the standard input stream. It is represented using *System.in*.

• **Standard Output** − used to output data produced by the user's program with the computer screen and used as the standard output stream. It is represented using *System.out*.

• **Standard Error** − used to output error data generated by the user's program with the computer screen and used as the standard error stream. It is represented using *System.err*.

Consider the example given below:

```java
import java.io.*;
public class ReadFromConsole {

    public static void main(String args[]) throws
IOException {
        InputStreamReader inp = null;

        try {
            inp = new InputStreamReader(System.in);
            System.out.println("Enter 'q' to quit.");
            char ch;
            do {
```

```
            ch = (char) inp.read();
            System.out.print(ch);
        } while(ch != 'q');
    }finally {
        if (inp != null) {
            inp.close();
        }
    }
  }
}
```

Compile the code from the command line and execute it. When prompted, type the letter '**q**' then hit the **enter** key. See what happens.

```
C:\Users\admin>javac ReadFromConsole.java

C:\Users\admin>java ReadFromConsole
Enter 'q' to quit.
q
q
C:\Users\admin>
```

You notice that once you press the letter '**q**' and hit the **enter** key, the program will quit.

You can run the code again and keep on pressing other letters and even numbers on the keyboard. Keep on pressing the enter key after every character you type. The program will only exit when you press the letter '**q**'.

This is showed below:

```
C:\Users\admin>javac ReadFromConsole.java

C:\Users\admin>java ReadFromConsole
Enter 'q' to quit.
h
h
e
e
r
r
1
1
2
2
4
4
q
q
C:\Users\admin>
```

Reading and Writing Files

We use the ***InputStream*** to read data from a source and ***OutputStream*** to write data to a destination. The most important streams for reading and writing files are the ***FileInputStream*** and ***FileOutputStream***.

The ***FileInputStream*** helps us to read data from files. We can create objects by use of the new keyword and we have access to a wide range of constructors. Consider the example given below:

```
InputStream f = new FileInputStream("F:/java/names");
```

In the above example, the constructor takes the name of a file as a string for creation of an input stream object for reading the file. Consider the next example given below:

```
File f = new File("F:/java/names");
InputStream f = new FileInputStream(f);
```

In the above case, we have a constructor taking a file object for creation of an ***input stream*** object to be used for reading the file. We have first used the ***File()*** method to create a file object.

Once you have created the ***InputStreamObject***, you are provided with several helper methods you can use for the purpose of reading the stream or perform other operations on it.

We use the ***FileOutputStream*** for the purpose of creating a file then writing some data into it. The stream will create a file if it is not found before it can be opened.

There are two constructors, we can use for the purpose of creating a ***FileOutputStream*** object.

The **first** constructor can be used as shown below:

```
OutputStream f = new
FileOutputStream("F:/java/names")
```

The constructor given above takes the name of a file as the string then creates an input stream object for writing the file.

The **second** constructor can be used as shown below:

```
File f = new File("F:/java/names");
OutputStream f = new FileOutputStream(f);
```

The constructor given above takes a file object for creating an output stream object for writing to a file. We have first called the ***File()*** method to create a file object. The following example shows how to use these:

```
import java.io.*;
public class FileStreamExample {

    public static void main(String args[]) {
```

```
    try {
        byte bWrite [] = {3,11,23,34,52};
        OutputStream os = new
FileOutputStream("myfile.txt");
        for(int p = 0; p < bWrite.length ; p++) {
            os.write( bWrite[p] );    // to write the
bytes
        }
        os.close();

        InputStream is = new
FileInputStream("myfile.txt");
        int size = is.available();

        for(int x = 0; x < size; x++) {
            System.out.print((char)is.read() + "   ");
        }
        is.close();
    } catch (IOException ex) {
        System.out.print("Exception");
    }
  }
}
```

Compile and run the code. It will generate a file named *myfile.txt* and it will write the specified numbers into that file. Note that the numbers will be written using a binary format. The output you get on the screen will also be in a binary format.

File Navigation

There are several classes in Java that can help us understand the concept of navigation.

File Class

This Java class represents both files and the directory *pathnames* in a hastily manner. It is the class we use for creating files and directories file deletion, file searching, etc. We use the file object to represent the real file/directory on the disk. The following example shows how we can create a *File object* and use it:

```java
import java.io.File;

public class FileExample {

    public static void main(String[] args) {
        File f = null;
        String[] strs = {"file1.txt", "file2.txt"};
        try {
            // for each string in string array
            for(String s:strs ) {
                // create a new file
                f = new File(s);

                // true for an executable file
                boolean bool = f.canExecute();

                // finding the absolute path
                String a = f.getAbsolutePath();

                // return the absolute path
                System.out.print(a);

                // to print
                System.out.println(" is executable: "+
bool);
            }
        } catch (Exception ex) {
            // in case an I/O error occurs
            ex.printStackTrace();
        }
    }
}
```

The code will get the directory of the files and tell you whether or not the files are executable.

FileReader Class

126

This is a Java class that inherits the ***InputStreamReader*** class. We use it for reading character streams. The class also comes with many constructors we can use for the creation of the objects we want. Here are the constructors provided with this class:

- **FileReader(File file)**- this is a constructor for creating a new reader when it is given the file from which it is to read.

- **FileReader(FileDescriptor fd)**- a constructor for creating a new *FileReader* when it has been provided with the *FileDescriptor* from which it should read.

- **FileReader(String fileName)**- this is a constructor for creating a new *FileReader* when provided with the file from which to read.

The following example shows how to use this class:

```java
import java.io.*;
public class FileReadExample {

    public static void main(String args[]) throws
IOException {
        File f = new File("hello.txt");

        // creating the file
        f.createNewFile();

        // creating a FileWriter Object
        FileWriter wr = new FileWriter(f);

        // Writing the content to file
        wr.write("A\n Java\n great\n example\n");
        wr.flush();
        wr.close();

        // Creating a FileReader Object
        FileReader fr = new FileReader(f);
        char [] ch = new char[50];
        fr.read(ch);    // read the content to an array
```

```
    for(char c : ch)
        System.out.print(c);    // print the
characters
        fr.close();
    }
}
```

The code will give the output given below upon execution:

```
C:\Users\admin>javac FileReadExample.java

C:\Users\admin>java FileReadExample
A
 Java
 great
 example

C:\Users\admin>
```

FileWriter Class

This is a Java class that inherits the *OutputStreamWriter* class. We use this class when we need to write streams of characters. The class comes with many constructors that can be used for the creation of objects. They include:

- **FileWriter(File file)-** this is a constructor for creating a **FileWriter** object when given the File object.

- **FileWriter(File file, boolean append)-** this is a constructor for creating a **FileWriter** object when given the File object having a Boolean that shows whether or not the given data should be appended.

- **FileWriter(FileDescriptor fd)-** this is a constructor for creating a **FileWriter** object that is associated with the file descriptor that is given.

- **FileWriter(String fileName)**- this constructor will create a **FileWriter** object when given the file name.

- **FileWriter(String fileName, boolean append)**- this constructor will create a **FileWriter** object when given the file name with a Boolean that shows whether or not the written data should be appended.

Here is an example showing how to use this Java class:

```java
import java.io.*;
public class FileReadExample {

    public static void main(String args[])throws
IOException {
        File f = new File("hello.txt");

        // creating the file
        f.createNewFile();

        // creating a FileWriter Object
        FileWriter wr = new FileWriter(f);

        // Writing the content to file
        wr.write("A\n Java\n great\n example\n");
        wr.flush();
        wr.close();

        // Creating a FileReader Object
        FileReader fr = new FileReader(f);
        char [] ch = new char[50];
        fr.read(ch);   // read the content to an array

        for(char c : ch)
            System.out.print(c);   // print the
characters
        fr.close();
    }
}
```

Listing Directories

To see all the directories and the files in a particular directory, you can use the *list()* method provided by the File object. This is showed using the following example:

```java
import java.io.File;
public class ReadDirectory {

    public static void main(String[] args) {
        File f = null;
        String[] paths;

        try {
            // creating a new file object
            f = new File("/tmp");

            // an array of both files and directory
            paths = f.list();

            // for every name in path array
            for(String path:paths) {
                // returns filename and the directory
name
                System.out.println(path);
            }
        } catch (Exception ex) {
            // in case any error occurs
            ex.printStackTrace();
        }
    }
}
```

17-Exception Handling

During the run-time of a program, an unexpected condition may occur which may stop its execution. We need to have a mechanism that will handle such conditions so that our programs will be executed without problems.

Problems that occur during the program execution are referred to as *exceptions*. Exceptions disrupt the normal flow of a program, and the program may not work as it was intended. Examples of exceptions that can occur during program execution include a case where the user enters an invalid data, a file that cannot open, loss of network connection during program execution, etc.

Consider the example given below in which we are trying to access a file that is not there:

```
import java.io.File;
```

```java
import java.io.FileReader;

public class ExceptionEXample {

    public static void main(String args[]) {
        File f = new File("F://hello.txt");
        FileReader fr = new FileReader(f);
    }
}
```

The code will give the following exception when compiled:

```
C:\Users\admin>javac ExceptionEXample.java
ExceptionEXample.java:8: error: unreported exception FileNotFoundException; must
be caught or declared to be thrown
        FileReader fr = new FileReader(f);
                        ^
1 error

C:\Users\admin>
```

Both the *read()* and *write()* methods have thrown the *IOException*, but the Java compiler could handle this together with the *FileNotFound exception*.

An unchecked exception is a kind of exception that occurs during the program execution time. Such exceptions are also referred to as *runtime exceptions*. Examples of such exceptions are *programming bugs* like improper use of APIs and logic errors. A good example of that is when you try to access an array element that is out of bounds as showed below:

```java
public class ArrayException {

    public static void main(String args[]) {
        int values[] = {10, 25, 38, 46};
        System.out.println(values[6]);
    }
}
```

In the above example, we have created an array of 4 elements, but we are trying to access the element at index 6 of the array. This will raise an ***ArrayIndexOutOfBoundsExceptionexception exception***.

There is a difference between ***errors*** and ***exceptions***. Errors are problems that occur and they are beyond the control of the programmer or the user. Errors are normally ignored in the code since there is nothing you can do about them. A good example of where an error can occur is after the occurrence of a stack overflow. Errors are ignored during compile time.

Catching Exceptions

To catch exceptions in Java, we combine the ***try*** and ***catch*** keywords. The code that is more likely to generate an error is surrounded using the ***try/catch block***. The code placed within the ***try/catch block*** is referred to as the protected code. Here is the syntax for using this statement:

```
try {
   // the protected code
} catch (ExceptionName ex1) {
   // the Catch block
}
```

After the occurrence of the exception, it will be handled by the ***catch block*** you have created. Anytime you create a ***try block***, it must be followed by either the catch or the finally block. If the exception that has occurred has been defined in the catch block, it will be passed to the catch block in the same way that an argument is passed to a method.

Here is an example:

```
import java.io.*;

public class ArrayException {

    public static void main(String args[]) {
        try {
            int x[] = new int[3];
            System.out.println("Access element four :" +
x[4]);
        } catch (ArrayIndexOutOfBoundsException ex) {
            System.out.println("Exception thrown   :" +
ex);
        }
        System.out.println("Outside the block");
    }
}
```

In the above example, we have defined an array with 3 elements but we are trying to access its **4th** element. The code will return the following result upon execution:

```
Exception thrown   :java.lang.ArrayIndexOutOfBoundsException: 4
Outside the block
```

Multiple Catch Blocks

We can create a try block followed by many catch blocks. This should be done following the syntax given below:

```
try {
    // the protected code
} catch (ExceptionType1 ex1) {
    // A Catch block
} catch (ExceptionType2 ex2) {
    // A Catch block
} catch (ExceptionType3 ex3) {
    // A Catch block
```

}

In the above syntax, we have created three catch blocks and a single try block. However, it is possible to use any number of catch blocks for a single try block. When an exception has occurred within the protected code, it will be thrown to the first catch block. If the exception's data type matches the **ExceptionType1**, then it will be caught there. If this doesn't occur, the exception will be thrown to the second catch block. This will continue for all the catch blocks in the code. If the exception is not caught, the method will halt the execution.

The following is an example of a code that shows how to use multiple catch statements:

```
try {
    f = new FileInputStream(file_Name);
    x = (byte) f.read();
} catch (IOException io) {
    io.printStackTrace();
    return -1;
} catch (FileNotFoundException ex) // Not valid! {
    ex.printStackTrace();
    return -1;
}
```

Throw/Throws Keywords

For a method that doesn't handle a checked exception, it must declare it by use of the **throws keyword**. This keyword should be added to the end of the signature of the method.

It is possible to throw an exception, which can be newly

instantiated or the one that you have just caught by use of the throw keyword.

It will be important to know and mark the difference between the *throw* and *throws keywords*. We use *throws keyword* to postpone the handling of an already checked exception while the *throw keyword* is used for explicitly invoking an exception.

Here is an example:

```java
import java.io.*;
public class ExceptionTest {

    public void save(double val) throws
RemoteException {
        // Implement the method
        throw new RemoteException();
    }
    // The rest of class definition
}
```

In the above example, we have the method *save()* which has declared that it is *throws* a *RemoteException*. It is possible for one method to declare that it will *throw* many exceptions, in which you should use commas (,) to separate the exceptions.

Consider the following example that shows how to implement this:

```java
import java.io.*;
public class ExceptionTest {

    public void save(double val) throws
RemoteException, InadequateFundsException {
        // Implement the method
    }
    // The rest of class definition
}
```

Finally Statement

The *finally block* comes after the *try* or *catch block*. This block will always be executed, regardless of whether or not the exception occurred. The final statement provides you with a good way of running your cleanup-type statements you need to be executed regardless of what happens inside your protected code. It should be added at the end of the *catch blocks* as showed in the following syntax:

```
try {
   //The protected code
} catch (ExceptionType1 ex1) {
   // A Catch block
} catch (ExceptionType2 ex2) {
   // A Catch block
} catch (ExceptionType3 ex3) {
   // A Catch block
}finally {
   // The finally block to always execute.
}
```

The following example shows this:

```
public class ExceptionTest {

   public static void main(String args[]) {
      int x[] = new int[3];
      try {
         System.out.println("Access element four :" +
x[4]);
      } catch (ArrayIndexOutOfBoundsException ex) {
         System.out.println("Exception thrown   :" +
ex);
      }finally {
         x[0] = 10;
         System.out.println("Element at index 0 is: "
+ x[0]);
         System.out.println("The finally statement
has been executed");
      }
   }
```

```
}
```

The code will return the following after execution:

```
Exception thrown  :java.lang.ArrayIndexOutOfBoundsException: 4
Element at index 0 is: 10
The finally statement has been executed
```

Note that java does not allow you to use a *catch clause* without the *try clause*. You don't have to add the *finally clause* to your **try/catch block**. And, you cannot use the *try clause* without either the *catch clause* or the *finally clause*.

Try-with-resources

After using resources like *connections*, *streams,* and others, we have to close them explicitly by using the finally clause. Let us show how you can open a file using the *FileReader* class and close the file by using the finally clause:

```java
import java.io.File;
import java.io.IOException;
import java.io.FileReader;

public class ReadandClose {

    public static void main(String args[]) {
        FileReader fr = null;
        try {
            File f = new File("colleagues.txt");
            fr = new FileReader(f); char [] c = new
char[50];
            fr.read(c);    // reads the content to the
array
            for(char ch : c)
```

```
            System.out.print(ch);    // prints the
characters one by one
        } catch (IOException ex) {
            ex.printStackTrace();
        }finally {
            try {
                fr.close();
            } catch (IOException ex) {
                ex.printStackTrace();
            }
        }
    }
}
```

The *try-with-resources* is a new way of handling exceptions in java and it automatically closes the resources that have been used within the *try* and *catch block*. To use the statement sets the resources that are required within parenthesis and the resources will be closed automatically at the end of the block. It takes the syntax given below:

```
try(FileReader fr = new FileReader("path to the
file")) {
    // the resource
    } catch () {
        // catch body
    }
}
```

Let us show how to use this statement to read data from a file:

```
import java.io.FileReader;
import java.io.IOException;

public class TrywithResources {

    public static void main(String args[]) {
        try(FileReader fr = new
FileReader("colleagues.txt")) {
```

```
        char [] c = new char[50];
        fr.read(c);   // to read the contents into
an array
        for(char ch : c)
        System.out.print(ch);   // to print
characters one by one
      } catch (IOException ex) {
        ex.printStackTrace();
      }
   }
}
```

For a class to use the ***try-with-resources*** statement, it must implement an ***AutoCloseAble*** interface and ***close()*** method which will be invoked automatically at run-time. Java also allows you to have multiple classes within a ***try-with-resources*** statement. If you do this, then the classes will have to be declared using a reverse order. The resource you declare in the try block will be instantiated before the beginning of ***try-block***. Other than the resources you declare within parenthesis, everything is similar to what we have in a normal ***try/catch block***. Any resource that you declare in the ***try*** will be instantiated before the beginning of the ***try-catch block***. Any resource declared within the ***try block*** will be implicitly declared as final.

User-defined Exceptions

Java allows you to create your own exceptions. However, any exception that you create should be a ***child of Throwable***. Anytime you need to create a ***checked exception*** to be automatically enforced by the ***Handle*** or set the rule, you should extend the Exception class.

To create our own *user-defined exceptions*, we use the following syntax:

```
class NewException extends Exception {
}
```

The above syntax shows that you are only required to extend the Exception class which is predefined so as to create your own exception. These are referred to as *checked exceptions*. Let us show how to create one in Java:

```
import java.io.*;

public class InadequateFundsException extends
Exception {
   private double deposit;

   public InadequateFundsException(double deposit) {
      this.deposit = deposit;
   }

   public double getDeposit() {
      return deposit;
   }
}
```

Now that we have defined the above exception, let us demonstrate how we can use it by writing an example:

```
import java.io.*;

public class AccountCheck {
   private double account_balance;
   private int number;

   public AccountCheck(int number) {
      this.number = number;
   }

   public void save(double deposit) {
```

```
        account_balance += deposit;
    }

    public void withdraw(double deposit) throws
InadequateFundsException {
        if(deposit <= account_balance) {
            account_balance -= deposit;
        }else {
            double needs = deposit - account_balance;
            throw new InadequateFundsException(needs);
        }
    }

    public double getAccountBalance() {
        return account_balance;
    }

    public int getNumber() {
        return number;
    }
}
```

Let us show how we can invoke the *save()* and *withdraw()* methods of the *AccountCheck* class:

```
public class BankExample {

    public static void main(String [] args) {
        AccountCheck c = new AccountCheck(101);
        System.out.println("Depositing $1000...");
        c.save(1000.00);

        try {
            System.out.println("\nWithdrawing $200...");
            c.withdraw(200.00);
            System.out.println("\nWithdrawing
$1100...");
            c.withdraw(1100.00);
        } catch (InadequateFundsException ex) {
            System.out.println("Sorry, your account is
short $" + ex.getDeposit());
            ex.printStackTrace();
        }
    }
}
```

Compile all the classes and run them. The exception should be raised at last as you will have withdrawn more from the account than what you have.

18-Java AWT

AWT stands for *Abstract Window kit* is an API that we use to develop window-based or GUI applications in Java. The components of Java AWT are platform-independent, meaning that these components are displayed based on the operating system. This API is heavyweight, meaning that its components use the resources of the operating system.

The *java.awt package* comes with many classes for the AWT api like *TextField, Label, RadioButton, CheckBox, TextArea, Choice, List*. Let us discuss some of its important components:

- *Container-* this is an AWT component capable of holding other components like textfields, labels, buttons, textareas, etc. it is extended by classes such as Frame, Panel, and Dialog.

- *Window-* this is a container with no menu bars and borders. To create a window, use a dialog, a frame or another window.

- *Panel-* this is a container with no menu bars and title bar.

You can add other components like textfields and buttons to it.

- *Frame*- this is a container with a title bar and it may have menu bars. You can add other components like textfields and buttons to it.

This class comes with differents methods, with the most important ones including the following:

- *public void add(Component c)*- this method adds a component to the component.

- *public void setSize(int width, int height)*- this method sets the measurements of the component, both the width and the height.

- *public void setLayout(LayoutManager m)*- this method defines the layout manager of the component.

- *public void setVisible(boolean status)*- this is the method we use to change the visibility of a component. It has a default setting of false.

We need to create an *awt* example. We need a frame for this. There are two ways through which we can create this:

- By extending the Frame class (inheritance).

- By creating an object of the Frame class (association).

Let us create our first example by inheriting the Frame class. We will add a button to the frame:

```java
import java.awt.*;
public class MyGui extends Frame {
MyGui() {
Button btn=new Button("click Here");
```

145

```
btn.setBounds(30,100,80,30);// set the button
position
add(btn);//add the button to the frame
setSize(300,300);// set frame size, 300 width, 300
height
setLayout(null);//no layout manager
setVisible(true);//make the frame visible, by default
it is not visible
}
public static void main(String args[]) {
MyGui mg=new MyGui();
  }
}
```

The code will return the following after execution:

We have used the **setBounds()** method to set the position for our button.

Let us now show how you can create *awt* by association:

```
import java.awt.*;
public class MyGui2 {
```

```
MyGui2() {
Frame fr=new Frame();
Button btn=new Button("click Here");
btn.setBounds(30,50,80,30);
fr.add(btn);
fr.setSize(300,300);
fr.setLayout(null);
fr.setVisible(true);
}
public static void main(String args[]) {
MyGui2 mg=new MyGui2();
}

}
```

The code should return the following graphical user interface:

Handling Events

An event refers to the process of changing the state of an object. Examples of events include a drag of the mouse button, a click of a button, etc. The Java package named *java.awt*.event provides many listener interfaces and event classes for handling events.

To handle events, you must register the necessary component with the Listener. If it is a button, for example, you want it to respond when clicked. In our previous examples, the button will do nothing when clicked. To register the component with the Listener, we normally call the *actionListener() method* as shown below:

```java
public void addActionListener(ActionListener a){
}
```

Now we have registered the component with the listener, we can add the event handling code. Consider the example given below:

```java
import java.awt.*;
import java.awt.event.*;
class MyEvent extends Frame implements
ActionListener{
TextField txtf;
MyEvent(){

//create the components
txtf=new TextField();
txtf.setBounds(60,50,170,20);
Button btn=new Button("click Here");
btn.setBounds(100,120,80,30);

//register the button with listener
btn.addActionListener(this);//passing the current
instance

//add the components then set their size, layout and
visibility
add(btn);
add(txtf);
setSize(300,300);
setLayout(null);
setVisible(true);
}
public void actionPerformed(ActionEvent event){
txtf.setText("This is a message");
}
public static void main(String args[]){
new MyEvent();
}
```

148

}

Once you execute the code, you will get the following interface:

The interface consists of a *textfield* and a button. Click the button and see what will happen. You will get the following:

When you click the button, some text is added to the *textfield*. The reason is that we added the code to add that text to the textfield on a click of the button. Let us see how we can handle events by an outer class:

Here is our first class, *MyEvent2.java*:

```java
import java.awt.*;
import java.awt.event.*;
class MyEvent2 extends Frame{
TextField txtf;
MyEvent2(){
//create the components
txtf=new TextField();
txtf.setBounds(60,50,170,20);
Button btn=new Button("click Here");
btn.setBounds(100,120,80,30);
//register with listener
OuterClass oc=new OuterClass(this);
btn.addActionListener(oc);//passing an instance of
outer class
//add the components then set the size, layout and
visibility
add(btn);
add(txtf);
setSize(300,300);
setLayout(null);
setVisible(true);
}
public static void main(String args[]){
new MyEvent2();
}
}
```

Here is the second class, *OuterClass.java*:

```java
import java.awt.event.*;
public class OuterClass implements ActionListener{
MyEvent2 mev;
OuterClass(MyEvent2 mev){
this.mev=mev;
}
```

```java
public void actionPerformed(ActionEvent ev){
mev.txtf.setText("This is a message");

}
public static void main(String args[]){
new MyEvent2();
}
}
```

Compile the first class, then compile and execute the second class. It will run as our previous example.

We can also handle events by using an anonymous class. Let us show this using an example:

```java
import java.awt.*;
import java.awt.event.*;
class MyEvent3 extends Frame{
TextField txtf;
MyEvent3(){
txtf=new TextField();
txtf.setBounds(60,50,170,20);
Button btn=new Button("click Here");
btn.setBounds(50,120,80,30);

btn.addActionListener(new ActionListener(){
public void actionPerformed(){
txtf.setText("This is a message");
}
});
add(btn);
add(txtf);
setSize(300,300);
setLayout(null);
setVisible(true);
}
public static void main(String args[]){
new MyEvent3();
}
}
```

AWT Button

We use the Button class to create a button with a label and this can be implemented on any platform. Action can also be added so that the button does something when clicked. The following shows how to use this class to create a button:

```java
import java.awt.*;
public class MyButton {
public static void main(String[] args) {
    Frame fr=new Frame("My Button");
    Button btn=new Button("Click Here");
    btn.setBounds(50,100,80,30);
    fr.add(btn);
    fr.setSize(400,400);
    fr.setLayout(null);
    fr.setVisible(true);
}
}
```

The code will return the following upon execution:

We can add the *ActionListener* to the button as follows:

```java
import java.awt.*;
import java.awt.event.*;
public class MyButton {
public static void main(String[] args) {
    Frame fr=new Frame("My Button");
    final TextField txtf=new TextField();
    txtf.setBounds(50,50, 150,20);
    Button btn=new Button("Click Here");
```

```
btn.setBounds(50,100,60,30);
btn.addActionListener(new ActionListener(){
public void actionPerformed(ActionEvent ev){
        txtf.setText("This is a message");
    }
});
fr.add(btn);
fr.add(txtf);
fr.setSize(400,400);
fr.setLayout(null);
fr.setVisible(true);
}
}
```

Run the code and click the button. The text will be shown in the text field.

A W T   L a b e l

The label object provides us with a way of adding text to the container. We use it to display one line of text which is read-only. An application can edit this text but the user may not change it directly. The following example shows how to create a label in Java:

```
import java.awt.*;
class MyLabel {
public static void main(String args[]){
    Frame fr= new Frame("My Label");
    Label lab1,lab2;
    lab1=new Label("Label 1");
    lab1.setBounds(50,100, 100,30);
    lab2=new Label("Label 2");
    lab2.setBounds(50,150, 100,30);
    fr.add(lab1);
    fr.add(lab2);
    fr.setSize(400,400);
    fr.setLayout(null);
    fr.setVisible(true);
}
}
```

The code should return the following interface when executed:

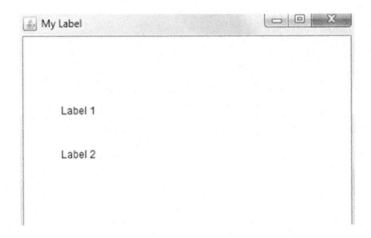

It is possible for us to add an action listener to a label. The following example shows this:

```
import java.awt.*;
import java.awt.event.*;
```

```
public class MyLabel2 extends Frame implements
ActionListener{
    TextField txtf;
    Label lab;
    Button btn;
    MyLabel2(){
        txtf=new TextField();
        txtf.setBounds(50,50, 150,20);
        lab=new Label();
        lab.setBounds(50,100, 250,20);
        btn=new Button("Find IP");
        btn.setBounds(50,150,60,30);
        btn.addActionListener(this);
        add(btn);
        add(txtf);
        add(lab);
        setSize(400,400);
        setLayout(null);
        setVisible(true);
    }
    public void actionPerformed(ActionEvent ev) {
        try{
        String host=txtf.getText();
        String
ip=java.net.InetAddress.getByName(host).getHostAddres
s();
        lab.setText("IP of host is "+ip);
        }catch(Exception ex)
        {
         System.out.println(ex);
        }
    }
    public static void main(String[] args) {
        new MyLabel2();
    }
}
```

Run the code then click the button. You should get both the name and the IP address of the current host, which is the host from which you are running the code:

AWT TextField

This is a component that allows a single line of text with the text being editable. It is inherited from the ***TextComponent*** class.

It can be created as shown below:

```java
import java.awt.*;
class MyTextField {
public static void main(String args[]){
    Frame fr= new Frame("My TextField");
    TextField txtf1, txtf2;
    txtf1=new TextField("Welcome to Java
Programming");
    txtf1.setBounds(50,100, 200,30);
    txtf2=new TextField("Java is a great coding
Language");
    txtf2.setBounds(50,150, 200,30);
    fr.add(txtf1);
    fr.add(txtf2);
    fr.setSize(400,400);
    fr.setLayout(null);
    fr.setVisible(true);
}
}
```

The code will return the result given below:

We have created two text fields with some text on them. Try and you will find that the text on the text fields can be edited. It is possible for us to add an action listener to a *textfield*.

Let us demonstrate this using an example:

```
import java.awt.*;
import java.awt.event.*;
public class MyTextField2 extends Frame implements
ActionListener{
    TextField txtf1,txtf2,txtf3;
    Button btn1,btn2;
    MyTextField2(){
        txtf1=new TextField();
        txtf1.setBounds(50,50,150,20);
        txtf2=new TextField();
        txtf2.setBounds(50,100,150,20);
        txtf3=new TextField();
        txtf3.setBounds(50,150,150,20);
        txtf3.setEditable(false);
        btn1=new Button("*");
        btn1.setBounds(50,200,50,50);
        btn2=new Button("+");
```

```
            btn2.setBounds(120,200,50,50);
            btn1.addActionListener(this);
            btn2.addActionListener(this);
            add(txtf1);
            add(txtf2);
            add(txtf3);
            add(btn1);
            add(btn2);
            setSize(300,300);
            setLayout(null);
            setVisible(true);
        }
    public void actionPerformed(ActionEvent ev) {
            String s1=txtf1.getText();
            String s2=txtf2.getText();
            int x=Integer.parseInt(s1);
            int y=Integer.parseInt(s2);
            int z=0;
            if(ev.getSource()==btn1){
                z=x*y;
            }else if(ev.getSource()==btn2){
                z=x+y;
            }
            String result=String.valueOf(z);
            txtf3.setText(result);
        }
public static void main(String[] args) {
    new MyTextField2();
}
}
}
```

The code will return the following interface after execution:

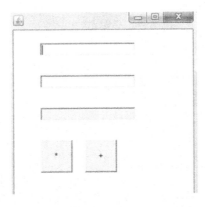

An interface is a simple form of a calculator. You can enter numerical values in the first two text fields then choose the operation you need to perform on the values from the two buttons at the bottom. In my case, I have entered 4 and 8. When I click the * button, I get the following result:

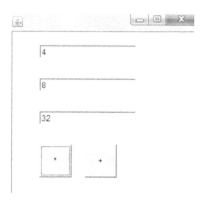

When I click the + button, I get the following output:

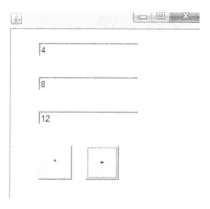

We have successfully added the action listener to the text field.

AWT TextArea

This is a multi-line text field used for displaying text. With this, the user may edit the text. It is inherited from the *TextComponent* class.

It can be created as showed below:

```java
import java.awt.*;
public class MyTextArea
{
    MyTextArea(){
        Frame fr= new Frame();
            TextArea ar=new TextArea("Welcome to Java
programming");
        ar.setBounds(10,30, 300,300);
        fr.add(ar);
        fr.setSize(400,400);
        fr.setLayout(null);
        fr.setVisible(true);
    }
public static void main(String args[])
{
    new MyTextArea();
}
}
```

The code will return the result given below after execution:

It comes with the text, we added to it within the code. However, it is possible for you to edit this text to what you want to have. We can also add an action listener to the text area. Let us show this:

```java
import java.awt.*;
import java.awt.event.*;
public class MyTextArea2 extends Frame implements
ActionListener{
Label lab1,lab2;
TextArea area;
Button btn;
MyTextArea2(){
    lab1=new Label();
    lab1.setBounds(50,50,100,30);
    lab2=new Label();
    lab2.setBounds(160,50,100,30);
    area=new TextArea();
    area.setBounds(20,100,300,300);
    btn=new Button("Count Words");
    btn.setBounds(100,400,100,30);
    btn.addActionListener(this);
    add(lab1);
    add(lab2);
    add(area);
    add(btn);
    setSize(400,450);
    setLayout(null);
    setVisible(true);
}
public void actionPerformed(ActionEvent ev){
    String txt=area.getText();
    String words[]=txt.split("\\s");
    lab1.setText("Total words: "+words.length);
    lab2.setText("Characters: "+txt.length());
}
public static void main(String[] args) {
    new MyTextArea2();
}
}
```

Run the code and enter some text in the text area. After that, click the *Count Words* button and see what happens. You will get:

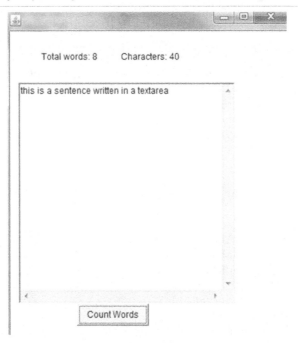

We have successfully added an action listener to the button.

AWT Checkbox

To create a **checkbox** in Java, we use the CheckBox class. The checkbox is used for turning an option to on *(true)* or off *(false).* When the checkbox is clicked, its state is changed to either on or off depending on its current state. Here is an example:

```java
import java.awt.*;
public class MyCheckbox
{
    MyCheckbox() {
        Frame fr= new Frame("My Checkbox");
        Checkbox cb1 = new Checkbox("Yes");
        cb1.setBounds(100,100, 50,50);
        Checkbox cb2 = new Checkbox("No", true);
        cb2.setBounds(100,150, 50,50);
```

```
           fr.add(cb1);
           fr.add(cb2);
           fr.setSize(450,450);
           fr.setLayout(null);
           fr.setVisible(true);
       }
public static void main(String args[])
{
    new MyCheckbox();
}
}
```

The code will return the following result once executed:

We can add an *ItemListener* to the checkbox as shown below:

```
{
     MyCheckbox2() {
         Frame fr= new Frame("My CheckBox");
         final Label lab = new Label();
         lab.setAlignment(Label.CENTER);
         lab.setSize(400,100);
         Checkbox cb1 = new Checkbox("yes");
         cb1.setBounds(100,100, 50,50);
         Checkbox cb2 = new Checkbox("No");
         cb2.setBounds(100,150, 50,50);
         fr.add(cb1);
         fr.add(cb2);
         fr.add(lab);
         cb1.addItemListener(new ItemListener() {
             public void itemStateChanged(ItemEvent
ev) {
                 lab.setText("Yes Checkbox: "
                 +
(ev.getStateChange()==1?"checked":"unchecked"));
             }
```

```
        });
        cb2.addItemListener(new ItemListener() {
            public void itemStateChanged(ItemEvent
ev) {
                lab.setText("No Checkbox: "
                +
(ev.getStateChange()==1?"checked":"unchecked"));
            }
        });
        fr.setSize(400,400);
        fr.setLayout(null);
        fr.setVisible(true);
    }
public static void main(String args[])
{
    new MyCheckbox2();
}
}
```

Run the code and you will get an interface with **Yes** and **No** checkboxes.

Try to check and uncheck the different textboxes and see the text you will get on the label:

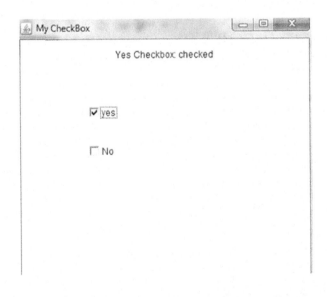

AWT CheckboxGroup

We usually create an object of the **CheckboxGroup** class to help us in grouping many checkboxes together. It is inherited from the object class. Only one checkbox should be in **"on"** state per group with the rest of checkboxes in the group being in **"off"** state. Here is an example:

```java
import java.awt.*;
public class MyCheckboxGroup
{
        MyCheckboxGroup (){
        Frame fr= new Frame("My CheckboxGroup");
         CheckboxGroup cg = new CheckboxGroup();
         Checkbox cb1 = new Checkbox("yes", cg,
false);
         cb1.setBounds(100,100, 50,50);
         Checkbox cb2 = new Checkbox("No", cg, true);
         cb2.setBounds(100,150, 50,50);
         fr.add(cb1);
         fr.add(cb2);
         fr.setSize(400,400);
         fr.setLayout(null);
         fr.setVisible(true);
      }
public static void main(String args[])
{
    new MyCheckboxGroup();
}
}
```

The code will return the following **Gui**:

You will realize that only one checkbox can be checked per time. We can also add an *ItemListener* to the *CheckboxGroup*. The following example shows this:

```java
import java.awt.*;
import java.awt.event.*;
public class MyCheckbox2
import java.awt.*;
import java.awt.event.*;
public class MyCheckboxGroup2
{
    MyCheckboxGroup2() {
        Frame fr= new Frame("My CheckboxGroup");
        final Label lab = new Label();
        lab.setAlignment(Label.CENTER);
        lab.setSize(400,100);
        CheckboxGroup cg = new CheckboxGroup();
        Checkbox cb1 = new Checkbox("yes", cg,
false);
        cb1.setBounds(100,100, 50,50);
        Checkbox cb2 = new Checkbox("No", cg, false);
        cb2.setBounds(100,150, 50,50);
        fr.add(cb1);
        fr.add(cb2);
        fr.add(lab);
        fr.setSize(400,400);
        fr.setLayout(null);
        fr.setVisible(true);
        cb1.addItemListener(new ItemListener() {
            public void itemStateChanged(ItemEvent
ev) {
```

```
                lab.setText("Yes checkbox: Checked");
            }
        });
        cb2.addItemListener(new ItemListener() {
            public void itemStateChanged(ItemEvent
ev) {
                lab.setText("No checkbox: Checked");
            }
        });
    }
public static void main(String args[])
{
    new MyCheckboxGroup2();
}
}
```

Run the code and click any of the checkboxes. You will see some text on the label.

The text will change when you click another checkbox:

We have successfully added an ItemListener to the checboxgroup.

AWT Menu and MenuItem

These are used for adding *menus* and *menu items* to the menu. This can be explained best by creating an example:

```java
import java.awt.*;
class MyMenu
{
    MyMenu() {
        Frame fr= new Frame("My Menu and MenuItem");
        MenuBar mnb=new MenuBar();
        Menu mn=new Menu("File");
        Menu smn=new Menu("Save");
        MenuItem i1=new MenuItem("New");
        MenuItem i2=new MenuItem("Copy");
        MenuItem i3=new MenuItem("Cut");
        MenuItem i4=new MenuItem("Save");
        MenuItem i5=new MenuItem("Save As");
        mn.add(i1);
        mn.add(i2);
        mn.add(i3);
        smn.add(i4);
        smn.add(i5);
        mn.add(smn);
        mnb.add(mn);
        fr.setMenuBar(mnb);
        fr.setSize(400,400);
        fr.setLayout(null);
        fr.setVisible(true);
}
public static void main(String args[])
{
new MyMenu();
}
}
```

Run the code and you will get a window. Click the File menu at the top left corner of the window. You will see several menu items under it. Click the Save option and see the submenus added to it:

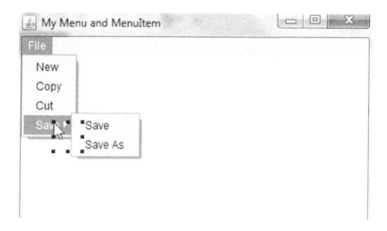

KeyListener Interface

The **KeyListener** will be notified after you have changed the state of the key. The notification is done against the **KeyEvent**. You can find the **KeyListener** listener in java.awt.event package.

The KeyListener interface has three important methods which include:

- **public abstract void keyPressed(KeyEvent ev);**

- **public abstract void keyReleased(KeyEvent ev);**

- **public abstract void keyTyped(KeyEvent ev);**

Consider the example given below:

```
import java.awt.*;
import java.awt.event.*;
```

```java
public class MyKeyListener extends Frame implements
KeyListener{
    Label lab;
    TextArea area;
    MyKeyListener(){

        lab=new Label();
        lab.setBounds(20,50,100,20);
        area=new TextArea();
        area.setBounds(20,80,300, 300);
        area.addKeyListener(this);

        add(lab);
        add(area);
        setSize(400,400);
        setLayout(null);
        setVisible(true);
    }
    public void keyPressed(KeyEvent ev) {
        lab.setText("Key Pressed!");
    }
    public void keyReleased(KeyEvent ev) {
        lab.setText("Key Released!");
    }
    public void keyTyped(KeyEvent ev) {
        lab.setText("Key Typed!");
    }

    public static void main(String[] args) {
        new MyKeyListener();
    }
}
```

Execute the code and try to type something with the textarea provided for you. You will see the text on the label change based on your action on the keyboard.

Conclusion

This marks the end of this book. Java is a coding language. It is popular for being one of the wide programming languages. A lot can be achieved with Java. It is good for the development of desktop applications, commonly referred to as standalone applications. It has applets, which can be added/embedded on web pages. It is easy to learn Java, especially with a background in object-oriented programming. Java supports features of object-oriented programming. Examples include polymorphism, classes, inheritance, encapsulation, etc. To code in Java, you need the Java compiler. This tells you Java is compiled, not interpreted. The compiler is installed automatically after installing JDK (Java Development Kit).

The JDK is open-source software, so get it for free and install it on your computer. A text editor is needed, which is where you will write your Java code. Examples include NetBeans, Notepad, Eclipse, etc. With those, you can write your Java codes and run them from the console/terminal of your OS. You invoke the java compiler (javac) to compile the code and generate a .class file, then execute the .class file. The .class file has byte-code, which is platform-independent, it can be run on any platform, example, Unix, Windows, Mac OS, Solaris, etc.

ABOUT THE AUTHOR

Daniel Bell was born in the Bronx, New York. When he was nine, he moved with his father Guy Bell to Nice in France. He received his Ph.D. degree in computer science from the University of Nice (France) in 2012. Daniel is conducting research in data management, with an emphasis on topics related to Big Data and data sharing, such as probabilistic data, data pricing, parallel data processing, data security. He spends his free time writing books on computer programming and data science, to help the absolute beginners in computer programming to code easily. He lives in Chatillon, near Paris.

Acknowledgments

Foremost, I would like to express my sincere gratitude to my family, my wife Genevieve and my son Adan for the continuous support in my everyday life, for their patience, motivation, enthusiasm. Besides my family, I would like to thank my friends and colleagues: Prof. Jule Villepreux, Hugo D. and Dr. James Rivera, for their encouragement, insightful comments, and hard questions. I thank my fellow labmates: Gang Yu, Ting Fan, Djibrilla Diallo, Juan Sanchez, for the stimulating discussions, for the sleepless nights we were working together before deadlines, and for all the fun we have had. Last but not least, I would like to thank my parents Guy Bell and Ezra Bell, for giving birth to me at the first place and supporting me spiritually throughout my life

GUZZLER
M E D I A

www.guzzlermedia.com

Made in the USA
Coppell, TX
31 May 2021